Hemi

The Ultimate American V-8

Robert Genat

CRESTLINE

This edition published in 2009 by
CRESTLINE
A division of Book Sales, Inc.
276 Fifth Avenue, Suite 206
New York, NY 10001
USA

Printed with permission and by arrangement with Motorbooks International.
First published in 2002 by Motorbooks, an imprint of MBI Publishing
Company LLC., Galtier Plaza, Suite 200, 380 Jackson Street, St. Paul, MN
55101, USA

Library of Congress Cataloging-in-Publication Data

Genat, Robert, 1945-
  Hemi : the ultimate american v-8 / By Robert Genat.
    p. cm.
  Includes bibliographical references and index.
 1. Internal combustion engines, Spark ignition. 2. Chrysler
automobile--Motors. I. Title.
TL210.G447 2007
629.222--dc22

2007018043

ISBN-13: 978-0-7858-2584-5
ISBN-10: 0-7858-2584-3

10 9 8 7 6 5 4 3 2 1

Editor: Amy Glaser
Designer: Katie Sonmor

Printed in Singapore

On the front cover: The 1971 'Cuda is one of the most sought after muscle
cars. It combines dramatic styling with the most powerful production muscle
car engine ever offered to the public.

On the frontispiece: In 1967, muscle cars had big engines, chrome wheels, and
red line tires. Plymouth's new GTX fit the mold perfectly—especially when
outfitted with the Hemi engine.

On the title page: The street Hemi engine brought a new level of performance
to Chrysler cars. Their muscle car credentials were confirmed by the Hemi's
wins on the nation's drag strips and on NASCAR's high-banked tracks.

On the back cover, top left: Chrysler's excellent LX platform provides the foundation for the Challenger concept. To preserve the proportions of the vehicle,
it had to be shortened by four inches.

On the back cover, top right: With only 14 vehicles built, the 1970 Hemi 'Cuda
convertible is one of today's most highly sought-after muscle cars. The new
1970 E-bodies came only in notchback and convertible body styles.

On the back cover, bottom right: All 1971 Hemi cars with the oval air filter
(except with the Shaker Hood) used a black "Hemi" decal on top with the
number "426" cut out of the "H." This engine compartment can be quickly
identified as a Road Runner by the purple horn in the foreground.

Author Bio:
Robert Genat is an accomplished author and photographer who has written
over 25 books for MBI Publishing Company, including a number of Mopar
muscle car histories. He and his wife, Robin, own and operate Zone Five
Photo. He lives in Encinitas, California.

CONTENTS

FOREWORD

By Bill Goldberg

Some remember their first kiss. I, on the other hand, remember my first ride in a Hemi car. As a sixteen-year-old kid, you are quite impressionable. At a time in my life when I had no idea what the word "Hemi" meant, boy, was I in for a treat. I believe it was a 1967 Coronet with yellow exterior and black guts. I had absolutely no idea what I was in for. And the power the car possessed was thrilling, to say the least. The brute force was astounding, and after that day, the word "Hemi" would be forever etched in my mind. After one ride, I was hooked. The sound, the smell, the feeling from riding in that car was something I had never experienced before. I knew that someday I would own a Hemi car.

When first becoming an aspiring car collector (junkie), I sought out what I thought were the coolest cars around—cars with character that, in their own way, went against the grain. The hunt was on! Holding onto my first childhood memory of riding in the Coronet, it seemed there was only one place to look—Mopar Land!

Fortunately, the success that I attained in wrestling and acting allowed me the opportunity to pursue my Hemi dreams. My first Mopar purchase was a 1968 GTX convertible from Texas, a 440 four-speed car. The second was a 1970 440 Six Pack 'Cuda from Salt Lake City. Finally in 1998, my dreams were realized. I stumbled across a 1969 Hemi Charger in Atlanta, Georgia. The Charger satiated my desire for the elusive Hemi, but why stop there?

Next was a 1970 Hemi Challenger that I located in 1999 in the upper Minnesota/Wisconsin area. The car was owned and raced by famed driver Al Corda. Though not a street car, I made numerous blasts down the runway at NASCAR driver Bill Elliott's race shop.

In 2001, I had yet another dream fulfilled. Since my 1969 Charger came not only with the original Hemi but a spare one to boot, I needed to find a new home for the "spare" Hemi. To make a very long story short, I purchased a 1970 Challenger convertible. Originally a 318 car, it was stripped, and two years later, I ended up with one of the meanest 1970 Challenger Hemi convertible cars around. Just how I would have ordered it from the factory.

Though the search intensified for the elusive Hemi car, it was not until a Barrett Jackson experience that I obtained the next one:

a red-red 1967 Hemi GTX, an original, one-paint car—I was in heaven. Since I first became a Hemi fan, I had always dreamed of owning one of the elusive lightweight super stock cars.

After searching for a number of years and not finding what I thought was the right deal, a twist of fate occurred. A gentleman approached me inquiring if I would like to participate in a Mopar "build-up." What a perfect platform for a monstrous super stock. After a little coaxing, I convinced him that a 1968 Dodge Dart would be the perfect car for the build. After major help from some major players, the car was completed in early 2006. Seven hundred and eighteen horsepower later, being fed through a monstrous Ray Barton Hemi, my Hemi super stock dreams had been realized.

What's next for the collection? Who knows! But in 2005, Chrysler did the unthinkable. They reinvented the modern day American muscle car with an updated version of the Hemi, bringing back their traditions of old. I've been lucky enough to be behind the wheel of a number of the SRT-powered vehicles. What a revival!—old-school power with modern styling and technology thrown in.

Though the new Charger Magnum and 300 are great additions to the modern muscle lineup, the gold at the end of my rainbow just might be the much-anticipated SRT Challenger. Yes, ladies and gentlemen, line up behind me because a new 2007 Challenger is on my list. From all the material I have seen, Chrysler has successfully reinvented this 1970 muscle car icon. With many of the major car companies concentrating on updating their 1970s iconic muscle lines, I do believe the 2007 Challenger will be the proverbial "cream" that rises to the top, rekindling the memories of old in a modern day package.

In *Hemi: The Ultimate American V-8*, Robert Genat captures the essence of three generations of the Hemi engine, from its roots as the powerplant for Chrysler's luxury cars of the 1950s, through the 1960s muscle car era, right through today's latest generation Hemi cars. Flipping through the pages, you can almost hear the roar, feel the power, and smell the tires burning. This book is a photographic cornucopia of what I believe are the coolest cars on the planet.

Bill Goldberg stands behind his latest Hemi car—a 1968 Dodge Hemi Dart clone. He preferred a clone to a rare original because he wanted a car he could drive anytime without worrying.

ACKNOWLEDGMENTS

I've often said that Hemi car owners are among the most eccentric of collectors. I say this with respect. These collectors own some of the most revered cars ever built; and by going to extremes to keep their special cars in top shape, they keep the Hemi mystique alive. Thanks to the following Hemi owners: Mel Mandel, Akbar Ali, Kenn Funk, Harold Sullivan, Mickey Weise, Ken Shrader, Mike Porto, Marlon Premo, Dan Norris, Earl Ortiz, David Mikkelson, Steve Atwell, John Hadgis, Steve Engel, Gil Garcia, Greg Joseph, Fred DeWitte Jr., Kirk Richardson, Emilio Parra, Anatol and Susan Vasiliev, and Bob Karakashian. Thanks to Hemi clone car owners and builders Walt Knoch, Joe McCaron, Brian Dickie, and Bob Mosher.

Thanks to drag racer Paul Rossi, and to Chrysler engineer Tom "Father of the Hemi" Hoover for their insights.

Thanks to Bill Goldberg for writing the foreword. Over the past year I have extensively photographed his large car collection, and we have become friends. It's because of his love of Hemi cars that I asked him to write the foreword for this book. Thanks, Bill.

In this book I've tried to include as many fully restored and unrestored original Hemi cars as I could find. A few of the original, unrestored cars have their share of dings, dents, and stone chips from three decades of driving. A few of the restored cars may even have some parts and components that may not be 100 percent stock. I forgive all Hemi owners for these non-stock modifications and especially those who have opted for radial tires or aftermarket wheels.

It should also be noted that production figures listed in this book are only as accurate as the sources I've used. I'm sure that a few Hemi-powered factory test cars and a few Hemi-powered Chrysler executive vehicles have made their way into circulation, skewing the accuracy of such published lists.

Thanks to the following DaimlerChrysler staff for all their help: Lori Dunning, Lisa Barrow, Scott Brown, Dan Knott, Bob Lee, Burke Brown, Micheal Castigione, Alan Barrington, and Brant Rosenbusch.

Thanks to fellow photographers and authors for their contributions: David Newhardt, Randy Leffingwell, Howard Kobe, Paul Herd, Dale Amy, and David Farrell.

I'd like to thank my editor, Amy Glaser, for her patience and good humor.

INTRODUCTION

A bolt of Hemi lightening struck on February 23, 1964, and the thunderclap it produced is still reverberating today. That lightening was first bottled in a blue 1964 Plymouth driven by a tall, lanky young man who would eventually become a legend in his own right. It wasn't long before many other drivers won races and became famous behind the wheel of Hemi-powered race cars. With Hemi power, races were won, careers were made, and ordinary men were transformed into heroes.

The Hemi engine, and the special cars in which it was installed, has endured fuel shortages, insurance surcharges, and the Japanese invasion of small fuel-efficient cars. Driving a Hemi car today is about as politically correct as whistling at a pretty girl on the street, but the people who own them could not care less. They love the massive look of the engine, the rump-rump idle, the axle-twisting torque it produces, and the miniscule numbers in which the cars were produced. No other automotive engine built has as much potential for horsepower as the Hemi. And no other muscle car produced is held in such high esteem as one that's Hemi-powered.

The Hemi engine is one of those unusual inventions with a special place in American automotive history. While Chrysler didn't invent the Hemi combustion chamber, they did perfect the Hemi and use it to its highest potential. First seen on the Welch passenger car at the turn of the twentieth century, the Hemi-design combustion chamber soon graced such mystical marques at Duesenberg and Stutz. Chrysler first got involved with the Hemi during World War II with experimental Hemi-style engines designed for tanks and aircraft. Between 1941 and 1945, Chrysler's Detroit Tank Arsenal produced 22,234 tanks and Chrysler's Chicago plant produced Wright Cyclone radial engines for the B-29 Superfortress.

Chrysler first introduced the Hemi in a production car in 1951. It displaced 331 cubic inches and produced 180 horsepower. The 1950s were a time in which much of the technology developed during World War II was put to use in designing and manufacturing consumer products. It was also an era of consumerism. There was a new enthusiasm for cars, houses, and other goods. The new Hemi engine fit perfectly into Chrysler's

INTRODUCTION

Continued

fresh automotive designs of the 1950s. The timing of the new engine was also important because it kept Chrysler on par with Cadillac and Oldsmobile, both of which released new overhead valve engines for their car lines.

At this time, Americans were also becoming interested in automobiles as more than a source of transportation. Automotive magazines were starting to pop up on the newsstands where enthusiasts could read road tests comparing their favorite models. Automotive competition of all types was brewing where enthusiasts could see how the cars fared head to head on the track or on an economy run. The Hemi proved itself well on the small dirt tracks of the South. Its only drawback was the heavy vehicle it was saddled with propelling. In 1957, the Automobile Manufacturer's Association (AMA) asked the automakers not to encourage racing. While Chrysler enjoyed the successes of racing, it didn't yet provide the advertising advantage that it would in a few years.

But the cost of producing the Hemi engine and developments in wedge cylinder head design no longer made it a viable choice for Chrysler's passenger cars. The Hemi was expensive to build and much heavier than any of the new wedge designs. Its true horsepower potential was also not being tapped into for passenger car use. When the early Hemi engine was discontinued at the end of the 1958 model year, it quietly disappeared as another chapter in the evolution of the automobile.

In the early 1960s, Chrysler was seen as an "engineering" automobile company. It was a place where "geeks" with slide rules on their belts from schools like MIT and Lawrence Tech went to work on bizarre intake systems, like the long-ram intake manifolds, unitized bodies, and push-button transmission controls. Chrysler's styling was also out of the mainstream in the early 1960s. The cars were a little on the "eccentric" side compared with their more traditionally styled Ford and Chevy counterparts. Today, the 1963 Dodge front end is seen by collectors as attractive and stylish, but in 1963 it was seen as out of sync with the styling themes of the day. As it turns out, Chrysler's styling and engineering were a step or two ahead of their time. That would come to bear in a few years.

Chrysler's interest in NASCAR racing pushed the development of new engines. Drag racing was seen as an "interesting" sport where Chrysler could also get involved. But the true potential of the drag racing customer was higher than that of the NASCAR fan. The drag racing customer was drawn into the dealer by the fast Super Stocks Dodges and Plymouths of the early 1960s. Unlike the 409 Chevys and 406 Fords, these Max-Wedge cars were fast right out of the box. The average drag racer could buy one and, with a little work, be relatively competitive on the strip and kick ass on the street.

But NASCAR, and especially the big 2 1/2-mile track at Daytona, was seen as the ultimate test of machinery. Chevrolet saw the writing on the wall and developed a new engine for the 1963 race. It's "Mystery 427" set records and put the competition into a tailspin. Unfortunately, it lacked the durability needed for a 500-mile race. The new engine's mechanical strength was not the only problem for competitors driving GM cars. Shortly after the 1963 Daytona 500, General Motors ceased support of all racing projects. With the field narrowed to two, Chrysler's task for 1964 was still formidable. Ford was dedicated to racing of all types and was prepared to spend whatever it took to win.

Chrysler also wanted to win and looked to the past for the engine of the future. The Hemi's wasted potential as a 1950s luxury car engine was about to change. The basic design of Chrysler's old Hemi head was adapted to a new generation of blocks. It had the horsepower and durability needed not only to win at Daytona, but dominate at racetracks everywhere. Automotive history was written in February 1964, and Chrysler would continue to do so on the high banks, short tracks, and drag strips for the rest of the decade.

Both NASCAR and NHRA wanted to encourage development of new engines, but they also wanted to see those engines available to all the competitors, not a select few. Rules were written to ensure the engines being raced were available, in some form, to the average car buyer. To comply, Chrysler introduced the Street Hemi in 1966. Unknowingly, Chrysler wrote another chapter in automotive history by providing the customer a race-bred engine in a detuned street version. Even when they were new, a mystique enshrouded the Street Hemi cars like a San Francisco fog. Ford, Chevy, and Pontiac produced some legendary muscle cars in the 1960s and early 1970s, but none had the long-lasting impact of the Street Hemi. And the engineering of the Street Hemi package was superb; there were no weak links. In addition, the wealth of options available allowed the Hemi buyer to build a personally tailored car around this marvelous engine.

Unfortunately, production of the Hemi ceased at the end of the 1971 model year. Insurance surcharges and new emission laws were the one-two combination that led Chrysler to throw in the towel. The heavyweight champ was forced into retirement.

The same mystique that drove people to the showrooms to buy Hemi cars also convinced them to hold on to them while the price of gasoline was rising. By the mid-1970s, a few were sold for pennies on the dollar and a few Hemi engines were pulled in favor of smaller, fuel-efficient engines. But many of the original Hemi cars were saved. They were stored in garages and barns because of the owner's little inner voice that told him that this car was something special and he wouldn't be sorry for saving it.

In 2005, the Hemi engine returned once again in a new form to provide outstanding performance and be the proverbial bur under the saddle of the other automakers. Chrysler initially selected a Hemi-designed V-8 as its replacement for the 3.6-liter truck engine. Certain criteria were established for this new truck engine: it had to be powerful, durable, provide room for growth, and be uncomplicated. After all the potential V-8 engine designs were evaluated, a Hemi concept was the one that met all of Chrysler's engineering goals. The third generation of the famous Hemi engine was born.

Chrysler now has three generations of Hemi engines. Each is unique in its design and application. The first version created a big statement for Chrysler's 1950s cars. While the cars of the 1950s were getting larger and heavier, the nation's network of roads was getting longer. The first-generation Hemi proved to be one of the most outstanding engines of the era. Drag racers realized the potential and quickly made the Hemi the engine of choice for serious drag racers. Hemi engines have carved a large niche in our automotive culture and into the souls of those who own 'em and love 'em.

CHAPTER ONE

THE AMAZING HEMI ENGINE

History has given the nod to the 1904 Welch four-cylinder engine as the first with a hemispherical combustion chamber to power a passenger car. The hemispherical combustion chamber was also used on Duesenbergs, Stutz, Miller, and Offenhauser engines. Over the years, the phrase "hemispherical combustion chamber" was shortened to Hemi. The name may have changed, but the design theory remained the same.

The combustion chamber on a Hemi engine is hemispherical. Cut a tennis ball in half and look at the inside. It forms the same shape as the hemispherical combustion chamber of a Hemi engine. No other shape can contain the same volume with as little surface area. This low surface-to-volume ratio improves the engine's volumetric and thermal efficiency, especially at speeds above 4,500 rpm. At these engine speeds, combustion time is at a minimum and the Hemi design works best to increase horsepower.

Another advantage to the Hemi design is the valve location—one on each side of the combustion chamber. This design allows for the shortest possible intake and exhaust ports and the largest valves. The flow-through design of the Hemi also contributes to valve cooling. Finally, the placement of the spark plug is almost dead center. All of these features are what make the basic Hemi design so good.

EARLY DEVELOPMENT

In 1965, the A-990 Hemi came with aluminum heads and water pump. The magnesium intake manifold was painted Hemi Orange and the valve covers were chrome-plated.

During World War II, Chrysler, along with the rest of the automotive industry, devoted itself to producing various types of mechanized war machinery. In addition to aircraft engines and trucks of all sizes, Chrysler led the nation in the production of tanks. Research and development into more efficient tank and aircraft engines led to experiments with the hemispherical combustion chambers. Before any production engines were developed, the war ended and Chrysler geared up for automotive production.

Chrysler's engineers continued to experiment with hemispherical heads. The first tests were performed on a single-cylinder engine. The horsepower gains with the hemispherical head were impressive when compared to other head configurations. Chrysler's results were contradictory to what the experts had been predicting. The hemispherical cylinder head did not induce detonation, and valve life was not compromised, as had been anticipated.

Encouraged by the results, the engineers designed a head to fit on one of Chrysler's production six-cylinder engines. This engine featured a Hemi head with chain-driven, double-overhead cams. This engine also ran smoothly. Unfortunately, the complexity of the double-overhead cams made a production version of this engine impossible. Designers tested a modified design that used pushrods.

In the late 1940s, Chrysler looked for new ways to power its new generation of cars. Their goal was to develop a more compact and powerful engine. Chrysler experimented with many different types of engines, including several V-6 engines, various inline six-cylinder designs, and even a five-cylinder inline design. A straight-eight was too heavy, and the current generation of inline six-cylinder engines did not have enough power. The new overhead valve V-8s of Oldsmobile and Cadillac were also on the horizon. The V-8 design provided a compact engine that was inherently smooth. Oldsmobile and Cadillac's decision confirmed that Chrysler's new engine had to be a V-8, and it was going to be a Hemi!

THE EARLY HEMIS

In 1948, Chrysler began testing a 330-ci Hemi-head engine. Extensive dynamometer tests were run to determine camshaft timing, ignition, and fuel curves. Road testing followed and confirmed that a hemispherical-head V-8 would launch Chrysler into the 1950s. The production version was coded A239. It was physically smaller and lighter than the prototype, but displaced 331 ci. This engine was also designed to be mass-produced. This first Chrysler Hemi V-8 would later take on the name Chrysler FirePower.

One of the design goals for the first Hemi engine was 100,000-mile durability. Engineers wanted to be sure that the major components would survive that many miles. One of the problems they faced was camshaft wear. Chrysler's engineers didn't have a lot of experience with overhead valve engines, especially one such as the Hemi, with its long rocker arms and higher-rpm ranges. Higher operating speeds required stronger valve springs, and the geometry of the rocker arm increased the pressure exerted on the camshafts by the lifter. The camshaft on some early test engines failed within hours. Engineers solved the accelerated wear problem by using new materials and a revised lubricant. Also slated for the new Hemi were hydraulic lifters. They would reduce routine maintenance and allow the engine to run quieter. The engine's shot-peened crankshaft with rolled fillets was a feature that extended its life.

The engineers used a sturdy block machined with close tolerances. Unusual to the first 331-ci Chrysler Hemi blocks was the extended bellhousing flange. This was used to accommodate the coupling for the Fluid Drive transmission. In 1954, when a new automatic transmission was offered, this extended flange was removed. The pistons used were cast-aluminum flat top with full floating pins. They used two compression rings and one oil ring. Below the oil ring was a horizontal expansion slot that was added to reduce piston slap when the engine was cold. The crankshaft, like all Hemi cranks, was forged steel. All Hemi cranks also featured eight flywheel/flex plate attachment holes. The large cast-iron Hemi heads were fitted with 1.81-inch intake valves and 1.50-inch exhaust valves that led to round exhaust ports.

Chrysler's first production Hemi engine was a 331-ci version that was installed in Chrysler cars. The FirePower was rated at 180 horsepower. This cut-away shows the complexity of the Hemi's valve train. *DaimlerChrysler Historical Collection*

One of the other design challenges was the location of the spark plug. The best location was in the center of the combustion chamber, but this location placed it between the rocker shafts, where access would be difficult. The problem was resolved with the use of flanged steel tubes. The bottom of the tube would double as a gasket for the spark plug. The top of the tube was flared with an o-ring that sealed against the surface of the valve cover. This required special ignition wires with an extended boot. These wires were hidden under a jacket that attached to the valve cover. To enhance drivability and performance, a special water-jacketed Carter carburetor with an automatic choke was used. A dual-point distributor was added to provide the hottest spark possible.

Following 8,000 hours of dynamometer testing and a half-million road-test miles, the new Hemi was ready for release. It was named FirePower and was rated at 180 horsepower. The first Chrysler cars to be equipped with the new Hemi were the 1951 Chrysler Saratoga, New Yorker, Imperial, and Crown Imperial. These were all high-profile cars in Chrysler's lineup and any failure of this new engine would shed an ominous shadow on Chrysler's ability to provide quality cars with superb engineering.

With 180 horsepower, the new FirePower Hemi provided a 14 percent increase in horsepower over the straight-eight engine it replaced. Better yet, it produced more horsepower than either Cadillac's (160) or Oldsmobile's (135) new overhead valve V-8s and didn't require premium fuel. The new engine made up for what Chrysler lacked in styling.

The success of the Hemi's introduction confirmed that the engine should be used in other Chrysler vehicles. Instead of using the same engine as Chrysler, the DeSoto and Dodge divisions decided to design their own engine with very few interchangeable parts (Plymouth never joined the Hemi brotherhood). This multiplicity of design and manufacturing was a major factor that contributed to the Hemi's high cost—and its eventual demise.

In 1952, DeSoto offered the FireDome, a 276-ci Hemi engine rated at 160 horsepower. It was installed in a new model that was also named FireDome. This new Hemi featured a 3.62-inch bore and 3.34-inch stroke. The intake valves were 1.75 inches in diameter, and the exhaust valves were 1.40 inches in diameter. This engine was smaller in overall dimensions and was 51 pounds lighter (669 vs. 710) than the Chrysler 331 Hemi. This 276 Hemi was also used in the 1953 FireDome DeSoto.

Most 1950s cars had extended engine compartments designed for the longer inline six- and inline eight-cylinder engines. The engine compartment of this 1953 Chrysler was large enough to handle the Hemi's physical size without any modifications. Water lines were run to the carburetor to regulate carburetor heat for drivability.

Dodge joined the Hemi club in 1953 with its 241-ci engine. The Red Ram was the smallest Hemi built by Chrysler in the 1950s and only weighed 590 pounds. It had a 3.44-inch bore and 3.25-inch stroke, with 1.66-inch-diameter intake valves and 1.40-inch-diameter exhaust valves. This engine provided power and economy. In the 1953 Mobilgas economy run, a Red Ram V-8 registered 23.4 miles to the gallon. This engine was carried over for the 1954 model year. Also offered in 1954 was a 150-horsepower version that gained the extra 10 horsepower with a half-point rise in the compression ratio to 7.5:1. An over-the-counter, dealer-installed Offenhauser four-barrel intake manifold was also available.

Chrysler removed the extended bellhousing flange from the back of the engine in 1954. Now all three divisions of Hemis had a common rear bellhousing mounting flange to match the new corporate automatic transmission. Chrysler's was also was the first Hemi to offer a factory four-barrel carburetor on its 331-ci Hemi in 1954. With this addition, the horsepower jumped to 235 and outpaced Cadillac's 230- and Oldsmobile's 185-horsepower V-8s. The horsepower race was getting into gear, with Ford introducing its first overhead valve V-8 in 1954; Chevrolet introduced its V-8 in 1955. Improved blends of premium gas allowed higher compression ratios and helped everyone move faster.

Chrysler redesigned its 331 Hemi for 1955. A new block was cast with revised water passages, and new heads were also cast with new water outlets. The new heads were designed without valve seat inserts like the previous heads had been. These heads also held larger 1.94-inch-diameter intake valves and larger 1.75-inch-diameter exhaust valves. A stamped front cover replaced the cast version used on the 1951–1954 engine. These changes, along with a boost in the compression, resulted in a 250-horsepower rating at 4,600 rpm. This engine was used in the new Imperial and the Chrysler New Yorker. The most impressive Hemi-powered 1955 Chrysler offering was the 300C. With dual four-barrel carburetors, the 300C's Hemi engine produced 300 horsepower. The best that Corvette could do that year was 195 horsepower, and Cadillac could only muster 236 horsepower out of its 1955 V-8.

A slight bore increase on DeSoto's 276 Hemi increased the displacement to 291 cubic inches for 1955. With a four-barrel, the FireDome Hemi engine was rated at 200 horsepower, and the two-barrel FireFlite version was rated at 185. Dodge also took the 241 Hemi engine to the boring bar and increased its

Each Chrysler model had its own distinct version of the Hemi engine. DeSoto used several names for its Hemi engines. This one is a 276-ci FireDome that was used in 1952 and 1953. It produced 160 horsepower and used a single two-barrel carburetor. The black stamping on the center of the valve cover shields the plug wires.

displacement to 270 cubic inches. The two-barrel version was rated at 183 horsepower and the four-barrel version was rated at 193 horsepower.

In 1956, Chrysler bored its 331 engine out to 3.94 inches. This increased the displacement to 354 cubic inches. With a 9.0:1 compression ratio and a four-barrel carburetor, this engine produced 280 horsepower. This engine was also used in the 1956 Imperial. In the stylish Chrysler 300, with a more aggressive cam profile, dual four-barrels, and 9.0:1 compression ratio, the Hemi produced 340 horsepower; with 10.0:1 compression it was rated at a whopping 355 horsepower. This was slightly more than one horsepower per ci—a magic number that engine designers had always viewed as the Holy Grail.

DeSoto offered three versions of the Hemi engine in 1956: two with 330-ci displacement and one with 341-ci displacement. The 341-ci Adventurer was equipped with dual quads and was rated at 320 horsepower. Dodge added a little stroke to its Hemi to increase the displacement to 315 cubic inches for 1956. The single four-barrel version was rated at 260 horsepower and the dual-quad version was rated at 295 horsepower.

Chrysler's last version of the Hemi design was released in 1957. It displaced 392 ci by way of a 4.00-inch bore and 3.91-inch stroke. The intake valve size was increased to 2 inches in diameter, while the exhaust valves remained at 1.75 inches. Compression on the 325-horsepower version was 9.25:1. The dual four-barrel version in the 300C was rated at 375 horsepower.

DeSoto offered its last Hemi engines in 1957. There were two 341-ci versions: the 270-horsepower FireDome, equipped with a two-barrel carburetor; and a FireFlite, equipped with a four-barrel, rated at 295 horsepower. DeSoto also had one 345-ci Hemi, named the Adventurer. The 4 extra cubic inches came by way of a .02-inch bore. Its compression ratio was one-quarter point higher than the two 241 engines and had dual four-barrel carburetors. Dodge also ended its Hemi production in 1957.

Like DeSoto, Dodge bored their 315 engine slightly to displace 325 cubic inches. The single four-barrel version was rated at 285 horsepower and the dual four-barrel version, listed as the Power Packoption, was rated at 310. For export models and racing, Dodge cleaned out its stock of the 1956 Chrysler 354-ci Hemis that had been used in the 300s. With dual four-barrel carburetors, these engines were rated at 340 and 355 horsepower.

Chrysler was the last to use the early Hemi engines in 1958 in its New Yorkers, Imperials, and 300Ds. The displacement remained at 392 cubic inches, but the compression ratio was raised to 10:1. With a single four-barrel, the engine was rated at 345 horsepower, and with dual quads in the 300D, it was rated at 380. There was also a short-lived Bendix electronic fuel injection unit that boosted the

Chrysler's first dual-quad installation was in 1955 on the 300C. The dual Carter four-barrels boosted the horsepower of the 331-ci engine to 300. The air cleaner is called a "bat wing" because of its unusual triangular shape. *DaimlerChrysler Historical Collection*

horsepower to 390. It proved to be too advanced for its day, and the few cars equipped with the unit were converted to dual quads. The cost of production and introduction of the new wedge engine was pushing the Hemi toward extinction. Also, the AMA's 1957 decree that automobile companies should refrain from actively supporting racing didn't help the Hemi's cause. When Chrysler ceased production of the Hemi at the end of 1958, the engine retired as the undisputed horsepower king of the 1950s.

THE RACE HEMI

The development of the wedge engine progressed quite well through the early 1960s. This engine performed well under the hood of a passenger car. It got reasonably good mileage and was less expensive to build than a Hemi. Even though NASCAR competition was heating up, the rule structure had changed in regards to production-type engines.

Chrysler's knight in shining armor was Lynn Townsend. He had two sons who frequented Detroit's Woodward Avenue and they let him know that the Chrysler's image was stodgy and the performance was equally as poor. It was at Townsend's request that performance was made part of the company's future programs. The 1962 413 Max Wedge was the first of the performance engines released under Townsend's leadership. It was

In 1956, the 330-ci DeSoto FireFlite Hemi engine was rated at 255 horsepower. It was one of three different Hemis offered by DeSoto that year. Because of the amount of hood room that 1950s era DeSotos offered, air cleaners were vertically stacked. Mounted on the back of the generator is the power steering pump.

followed by the 1963 426 Max Wedge engines, both of which were used in NASCAR and drag racing.

On the strip the Max Wedge engines were the class of the field, but on the NASCAR ovals, the engines didn't have a stellar record. In the spring of 1963, Townsend asked, "What would it take to win the NASCAR Daytona race in February 1964?" If a fundamental change in engine design was in order, the race engine group, headed by Bob Hoover, had the most experience in high-output versions of the Hemi. "If you want to go there and go like stink let's adapt the Hemi head to the race B engine," Hoover said.

The project was approved in April 1963. It was an ideal program. The designers and engineers were enthusiastic about what they were doing and top management fully funded the program. Management's support came from the fact that the wedge programs had been so successful and they were hot to win Daytona. "We had an idea from the old A-311 (Indy Hemi engine) program what kind of port areas we wanted and how to design a connecting rod that would take the heavy piston weight of the Hemi," recalls Hoover.

The previous A-311 Hemi design also gave the engineers a clue as to the general valve timing that worked best. "The early Hemis were a guiding light as to where we wanted to go," says Hoover. The new Hemi's bore was limited by the bore centers allowed in the Trenton engine plant. This was an old Packard engine plant with machinery that had limited capability. The included valve angle was the same as the A-311 engine. Because of the limited time available, Chrysler's engine team used the fundamental engineering rule that more horsepower could be produced by intensive development of an existing design, than what could be achieved by starting over with a completely new design.

In April 1963, Frank Bilk was assigned to do the layout of the head and the valve gear. "I've been called the father of the Hemi, but Frank was the real father of the Hemi—I just provided some ideas," Hoover said. Hoover also said that Bilk had a gift of visualization, something every great designer must have.

Designers made the decision to make the exhaust rocker arm the same length as the one on the 392 Hemi engine. It was the longest and heaviest of the rocker arms available at that time. Hoover knew that Top Fuel dragster racers were running the 392 engine at speeds as high as 7,000 rpm. Making radical changes to that key component, rocker arms, might have jeopardized the engine's ability to reach high rpms. Bilk was also the one who tipped the entire head inboard a few degrees to allow the exhaust pushrod to clear the head gasket bead. This also enhanced the flow line to the intake valve.

The only penalties of this design included a slight increase in the surface area of the combustion chamber and the shape of the

Left
The air cleaner has been removed from this 1956 Imperial's 354-ci Hemi engine to reveal the Carter four-barrel carburetor. This 280-horsepower FirePower engine is the same engine installed in Chrysler cars that year.

Right
The lower hood line of the 1957 Chrysler 300C required these unique air filters for the dual Carter carburetors. Each carburetor also had an external fuel filter with a glass sediment bowl.

Funny Cars emanated from the Dodge and Plymouth Super Stock ranks during the 1965 drag race season. Many owners switched to Hilborn fuel injection and ran alcohol or nitromethane for fuel.

Left
When the 426 Hemi was introduced in 1964, it was offered in three versions: a single four-barrel 400-horsepower version for NASCAR, and two dual-quad versions at 415 and 425 horsepower. This 1964 Dodge is equipped with a 415-horsepower Hemi. The large chrome air cleaner was standard with the dual-quad, but most owners discarded them when the car was raced. All 1964 Hemis came with chrome valve covers.

exhaust port. Chrysler sent models of the exhaust ports to Harry Westlake in England. He optimized them by revising the shape. Back at Chrysler, Hoover gives credit to Forbes Bunting for his work on the new Hemi's intake manifolds.

Once the basic design work was completed, it was a rush to get prototype engines built for testing. The blocks were cast and machined at Chrysler's Trenton, Michigan, engine plant. The first engines were built at the Chrysler engine lab in Highland Park. It took 80 man-hours to assemble each of the first Hemi engines because of the care given to inspecting and checking critical tolerances.

Early dyno testing revealed a weakness in the right-hand cylinder walls that led to cracks. Because of the deadline for the Daytona race, competitors were sent blocks that Chrysler knew would not be race worthy, but could be used for inspection and

When the street Hemi was released in 1966, the valve covers were painted with black crinkle paint and the large air cleaner was chrome-plated. One small "426 Hemi" decal was placed on the front of the air cleaner. The color of the street Hemi engine was red-orange, as opposed to the brighter hue of the race Hemi's orange.

qualifying purposes. New, more durable blocks were delivered just days before the race. A Hollywood screenwriter couldn't have done a better job of scripting the outcome of the 1964 Daytona 500. Chrysler's Hemi became the king of NASCAR's hill and would retain its position for years to come.

The drag racing version of the Hemi was not released in February 1964, when the NASCAR version was introduced. This handed the Super Stock class over to the new Ford Thunderbolts at the NHRA Winternationals in Pomona. The Chrysler wedge-equipped cars had their way, however, in the Super Stock Automatic class. The Hemi cars were not released to competitors until mid-1964.

When first released, there were two versions of the engine for drag racing. The 415-horsepower version featured 11:1 compression and dual Carter AFB carburetors on the cross-ram intake. This engine, of which there were few, was only fitted to steel-bodied cars. The lightweight aluminum cars received the 425-horsepower version that had 12.5:1 compression and Holley carburetors. Both of these engines had a cast-iron exhaust flange with tubular headers.

Paul Rossi was a young drag racing competitor who lived in the Detroit area in the shadow of the two factory race teams: the Golden Commandos and the Ramchargers. His 1963 Max Wedge Plymouth was wildly successful, and for his efforts as an independent, he received a new 1964 Plymouth Hemi car. Unfortunately, he didn't receive his Hemi car until June. "We were supposed to get the car in January, but when we tested, my 1963 Wedge car continually kicked the shit out of the Hemi on the track," Rossi said. The release of the drag race versions was delayed until Chrysler was sure that the engines would be measurably better than the Max Wedge engine. One of the key components to the improvement of the Hemi for drag racing was a new camshaft.

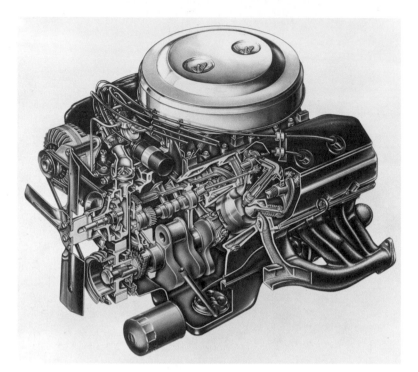

Above
The street Hemi engine was fitted with a streamlined set of cast-iron exhaust manifolds when it was first installed in 1966. This right-hand side manifold has a heat control valve that directs heat to the intake manifold when the engine is cold.

Left
The exhaust manifold on the left side of the street Hemi engine was required to take a quick turn at the front to clear the steering gear. This engine is being assembled on its K-member just before installation.

In 1967, federal vehicle laws required a closed crankcase system and a dual master cylinder. The longer master cylinder and the addition of an optional power brake booster made removal of the left valve cover difficult. This design problem was alleviated by the fact that one could remove the booster assembly from the engine compartment: this was a feature unique to Hemi cars.

When Rossi finally got his new Hemi car, he was concerned that it wouldn't be as fast as his Wedge car. He was also told that if he lived anywhere outside the Detroit area, he would receive a lot more support from the factory because Detroit had two factory teams. This was the start of Chrysler's Direct Connection program, where Chrysler directly supported the racers with free parts. "I would go down and pick up a set of gaskets, a camshaft, lifters, and some valve springs," recalls Rossi. "That was a hell of a deal!" The free parts were on a "need-to-have" basis in order to replace a broken component. Participants would also be given the latest factory-proven components. "If I lost a transmission or an engine, I could call them and get another one," says Rossi.

Rossi successfully ran his Hemi car for the balance of the 1964 season and switched to a Mercury Comet in 1965. Toward the end of the 1964 season, a few competitors started to "adjust" the wheelbase of their cars for better traction. This trend would continue in 1965 and eventually would lead to some exotic-looking race cars.

Chrysler targeted the 1965 NHRA Super Stock class with specially built Dodges and Plymouths, which were known as A-990 cars. The bodies were lightweight and the engine was a specially built race Hemi. Fitted with aluminum heads, A-990s were only available with a 12.5:1 compression ratio. The intake manifold for the A-990s was the same basic design as the one used on the drag cars in 1964, except the material of choice was now magnesium.

Unique to the 1965 A-990 Hemi engine was an aluminum water pump and an aluminum oil pump. The camshaft for the 1965 A-990 had 312 degrees of duration. These cars were successful from the first day they ran. At the 1965 NHRA Winternationals, the

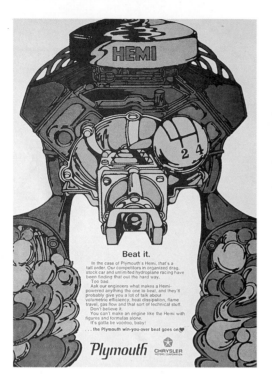

Plymouth was never shy about tapping into popular culture for its advertising campaigns. Its "The Beat Goes On" theme song was originally a 1967 hit song by Sonny and Cher. The colorful graphic style of the artwork was derivative of 1960s pop artist Peter Max.

Super Stock field was composed entirely of A-990 cars. Coming out on top was Plymouth driver Bill Jenkins, who ran an elapsed time of 11.39 seconds at a speed of 126.05 miles per hour in the final run. These engines were also installed in the altered-wheelbase A/FX cars Chrysler built in 1965.

With the release of the street Hemi in 1966, Chrysler eliminated its special drag race cars. Drag racing competitors used street Hemis in A/Stock class, and the older A-990 still qualified for Super Stock. The cars competing in A/Stock were equipped with production 426 street Hemi engines. A revised intake manifold was new for NASCAR competition in 1966. Nicknamed "the bathtub" because of its unusual shape, it was a plenum-style intake for a single four-barrel carburetor. The other change required by NASCAR was to reduce the stroke on the version used for long, high-speed tracks. A crankshaft with a stroke of 3.56 was installed, which reduced the displacement to 404 cubic inches. This did little to slow down the Hemi.

In 1967, Dodge and Plymouth each built 55 cars for NHRA's SS/B class. They were lightweight cars specifically built for that class. The engines were unmodified production-line street Hemis. The last race Hemis produced for drag racing were part of a small series of 1968 Dodge Darts and Plymouth Barracudas. Hurst built 75 of each for Super Stock competition. Like all the other Hemi cars, these cars were very successful and many are still being raced today.

In 1969 and 1970 Chrysler made several different heads for NASCAR use. They had modified ports, larger valves, and some were cast in aluminum. Much of this design work on heads went into the Pro Stock effort, which began in 1970.

Chrysler's racing effort, especially in the Hemi years, was well planned and executed with precision. The team developing the engine learned a lot with the Max Wedge program and applied that knowledge and the lessons learned on the early Hemis to the new generation of race Hemis. The greatest tribute that can be paid to these engineers is the longevity of the Hemi and its ability to consistently win races.

THE STREET HEMI

The street Hemi came about as a result of the proliferation of high-performance street cars in the mid-1960s, and due to the need to have a production version of the engine, Chrysler wanted to race on the NASCAR tracks. An internal memo was cowritten by Special Car Manager Bob Roger, and Chief Engineer Robert Cahill on January 6, 1965. It was addressed to J. C. Guenther, manager of styling, and H. R. Steding, executive engineer. It outlined the format for a detuned Hemi for B-body cars. Roger and Cahill suggested an engine with dual four-barrel carburetors, cast-iron exhaust manifolds, cross-bolted main bearing caps, and an intake manifold and camshaft that would provide ample power, but maintain driveability in winter and summer. They preferred a hydraulic cam, but said solid lifters would be acceptable. They also wanted thermally controlled pistons to reduce noise when the engine was cold. The engine was to be developed for both four-speed and automatic transmissions. They stipulated no air conditioning and no limited warranty. They projected 1966 sales to be between 5,000 and 7,000 units. W. J. Bradley issued a product description and made it official on January 12, 1965. There would be a street Hemi for 1966.

Only a few changes were made to the Hemi block's mounting lugs. The crankshaft and the rods were the same as those used on the A-990 race cars. The camshaft was smoothed out, in comparison to the race version, with a relatively mild 276 degrees of duration. The valves, mechanical lifters, pushrods, and rocker arms were straight from the race engine. Because the engine would run in lower maximum-rpm ranges than the race engine, the valve spring rates were lowered. This also guaranteed extended camshaft life.

The new street Hemi bowed to the history of dual-quad intake manifolds on Chrysler's performance Hemis of the past. The new intake manifold was cast from aluminum and was a dual-plane design. It mounted two Carter AFBs: 4139S in the front and 4140S in the rear. The rear carburetor was the primary with a choke, and

Above

Between 1968 and 1970, cars equipped with the round chrome air cleaner, such as this 1969 Charger, received a new semicircular decal that stated "426 Hemi Head." The last Hemi car to use this type of air cleaner was the 1970 Dodge Charger.

Left

When Chrysler shoehorned the race Hemi into the 1968 A-body Darts and Barracudas, they had to make a special mount to move the master cylinder outboard to clear the valve covers. This was the last time a race Hemi engine was installed in a vehicle produced by Chrysler.

The only intake manifold used on the street Hemi engine was this one that mounted dual Carter AFBs. It was made of aluminum and was mounted on the engine prior to painting, hence the orange paint.

The hemispherical combustion chamber is where the street Hemi's power is made. It is fully machined and uses a 2.25-inch-diameter intake valve and 1.94-inch-diameter exhaust valve.

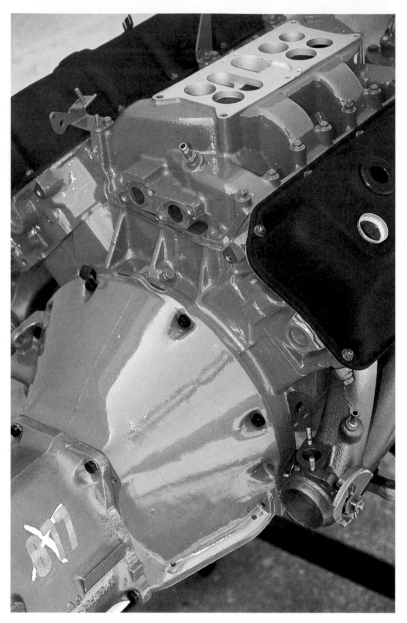

Street Hemis used a unique bellhousing that contained a steel flywheel. The standard clutch-plate diameter is 11 inches. The two holes in the back of the intake manifold are for heat tubes from the exhaust.

the front carburetor was the secondary without a choke. They were linked with a mechanical staged linkage that allowed all routine street driving to be done on the rear carburetor.

When the throttle was approximately 2/3 to 3/4 depressed, the front carburetor would start to open. With the accelerator fully depressed, both carburetors would be fully open. To prevent stumbling when both carburetors were fully open at low engine

speed, Carter AFBs used a secondary air valve that precisely tailored carburetor airflow capacity to the engine's requirements. The Carter AFBs were simple, but efficient, carburetors.

Only a few minor changes were made to the heads in order to mount the large cast-iron exhaust manifolds. Because of the size of the Hemi's five-quart oil pan, an 8-inch-wide plate was added to the K-member to protect it from road damage. Black crackle paint was slated for the street Hemi's valve covers and air cleaner. By the time the first production street Hemis were released, the large round air cleaner was chrome plated. A small decal with silver and black letters on an orange background that read "426 Hemi" was atop the air cleaner.

A new, cast-iron bellhousing was made for the street Hemi's 11-inch clutch. Only two transmissions were slated for the new engine: the A833 four-speed manual and the heavy-duty A727 TorqueFlite. This transmission used five discs and the second gear band was increased in size from 2.0 to 2.5 inches. Each of the street Hemi engines was built at the Marysville, Michigan, plant. Every engine was carefully built and inspected. The dyno tests proved that the engine could consistently produce 425 horsepower. Everyone knew that these engines would be hammered hard and tested to their limits by the young Turks who wanted to emulate Dick Landy and Ronnie Sox. Any failures would hurt the overall Hemi program, as well as Chrysler's reputation.

The new street Hemi was installed into Dodge and Plymouth 1966 B-bodies and the new Dodge Charger based on the B-body. The cost of the Hemi option in a new Plymouth Satellite was $1,105. A Satellite equipped with a V-8 listed for $2,810. To order a Hemi in 1966, you either had to be wealthy or love serious horsepower. A total of 2,731 Dodge and Plymouth vehicles were sold with Hemi engines in 1966, with Plymouth Satellite hardtops recording the most installations at 817. These numbers fell far short of product planning's predictions of 5,000 to 7,000 units.

Hemi sales in 1967 were even more disappointing. Making things more difficult for the Hemi was that it was competing internally against the new, reasonably priced, 440-ci engine. The Hemi engine was mechanically unchanged for the 1967 production year. The 110 cars built for Super Stock competition were even equipped with a standard production-line Hemi. That alone says volumes about Chrysler's faith in the Hemi.

Beginning in 1969 and continuing through the end of production, Plymouth B-body Hemis, including this Road Runner, were equipped with an Air Grabber system. It was called a Ramcharger on Dodge B-bodies. This system included an oval-shaped, open-element air filter and an underhood, fresh-air ductwork that attached to a hood scoop opened by a vacuum solenoid. On top of the air cleaner lid is a "Coyote Duster" decal.

The exception to the B-body Air Grabber rule was the 1970 Road Runner Superbird. It did not have an Air Grabber system or decal on the air cleaner lid.

In 1970 and 1971, the Shaker Hood scoop was standard on Hemi 'Cudas and optional on Hemi Challengers. This large device contained the air filter element and a cable-operated door. Most Shaker scoops were painted a low-gloss black, but they could also be ordered in body color with certain color selections.

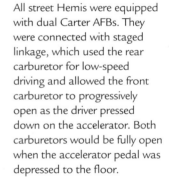

All street Hemis were equipped with dual Carter AFBs. They were connected with staged linkage, which used the rear carburetor for low-speed driving and allowed the front carburetor to progressively open as the driver pressed down on the accelerator. Both carburetors would be fully open when the accelerator pedal was depressed to the floor.

The 426-ci street Hemi engine was first released in 1966 as an option in B-body Plymouths and Dodges. It was initially offered to comply with NASCAR's ruling requiring a production-based engine. The biggest change in its six-year production run was the change to the hydraulic lifter cam in 1970. *DaimlerChrysler Historical Collection*

Dodge and Plymouth offerings were both restyled for 1968. This change drew buyers back into the showrooms and into the Hemi brotherhood. The engine was again unchanged, except for a slight modification to the camshaft profile. The only change in 1969 was made to the air cleaner. All Hemi-optioned cars, with the exception of the Dodge Charger, were equipped with some type of cold-air induction system. On Plymouths, it was called Air Grabber, and on Dodges, it was named Ramcharger. This change did not affect horsepower ratings.

The biggest modification to the street Hemi during its short existence was a change to the hydraulic cam in 1970. This relieved the owners of the difficult task of adjusting the lifters. To adjust the lifters on a Hemi with power steering necessitated the removal of the brake booster in order to remove the left valve cover. The booster also had to be removed to reach the rear spark plug on the left side.

The valve adjustment specifications called for the Hemi to be adjusted cold with the lifter on the base circle of the cam. Lash for intake is .028 and exhaust is .032. Also new for 1970 on Hemi 'Cudas and Hemi Challengers was the Shaker Hood scoop, although it was optional on the Challenger. Like the Ramcharger

Left
All 1971 Hemi cars with the oval air filter (except with the Shaker Hood) used a black "Hemi" decal on top with the numbers "426" cut out of the letter "H." This engine compartment can be quickly identified as a Road Runner by the purple horn in the foreground.

and Air Grabber systems, the Shaker Hood scoop had no effect on horsepower ratings. It just looked cool.

The street Hemi was produced in limited numbers for six short years. Those years constituted the peak of the muscle-car era and the Hemi was at the top in power and availability. The Hemi was expensive and required more care than the average V-8 engine. One can only imagine the impact on the market if the street Hemi had been produced from day one with hydraulic lifters and a single four-barrel carburetor at a cost of $300. Part of the fascination with the Hemi is the fact it was an expensive, aggressive engine that was produced in limited numbers.

The Chrysler Hemi engine stands alone in the field of pushrod engines due to the amount of power it can produce and because of its rarity. It's true that many of today's multivalve overhead cam engines can produce more horsepower per cubic inch, but those engines are the result of years of research and development. They also have the advantage of overhead cams and multiple valves per cylinder. Today's engines were also developed using advanced materials, sophisticated computer programs, and high-tech testing equipment. The Hemi was designed with paper, pencils, slide rules, and lots of common sense. It was also created by a small team of engineers who were given a mission and then left alone to accomplish that task without endless meetings and meddling from upper management. In combination with some of the most imaginative and beautiful styling ever seen, the Hemi engine left an indelible mark on automotive history.

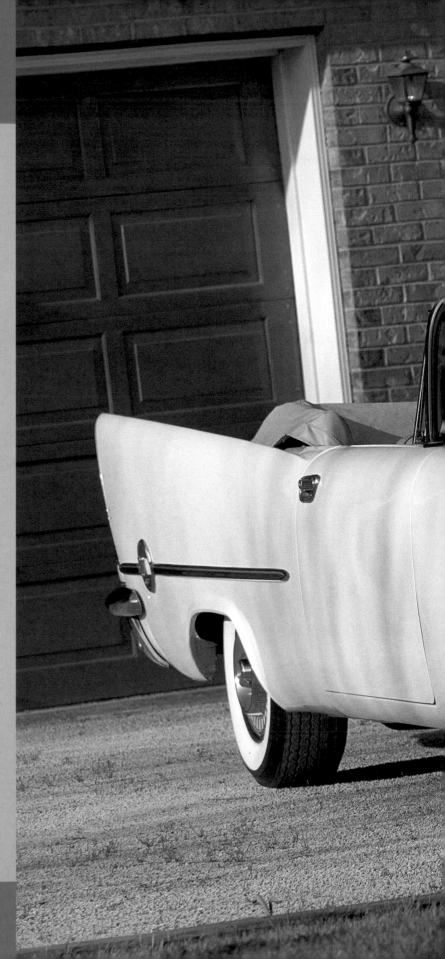

CHAPTER TWO

EARLY HEMI CARS

1951–1958

The 1950s was a marvelous time in the auto industry: the economy was strong and buyers were eagerly looking forward to the new models. The cars of the late 1940s were rehashed prewar designs that offered little technical innovation or daring style. They were new and they were cars, but they weren't what the public was looking for.

As the 1950s dawned, much of the technology and ingenuity that had won the war were starting to appear in the automotive industry. Cars took on the shape of fighter aircraft, such as the twin-tailed P-38. Powerful overhead valve V-8 engines, similar in design to the V-12 Allison that powered the P-38, were also being produced. Cars were no longer just a means of transportation; a car became an extension of an individual's personality, a luxury previously reserved for only the very rich. In the 1950s, there was a new car with appeal for everyone.

Chrysler's cars of the late 1940s were boring boxes that lacked style, and sales were starting to decline. Then Chrysler President K. T. Keller favored the practical rather than the stylish. Luckily, Keller left the company in 1950 and his successor was Lester "Tex" Colbert. Colbert planned a complete redesign of all Chrysler models and the elimination of the six-cylinder engine by 1954. Legendary designer Virgil Exner, who joined Chrysler in 1949, helped Colbert reach his

The decade of the 1950s was a marvelous time for Chrysler. Virgil Exner's styling set trends, and the powerful Hemi engine set records. This stylish 1957 Chrysler 300C convertible is powered by a 392-ci, 375-horsepower Hemi engine. This was the first year a 300C was offered as a convertible. ©Dale Amy

In 1953, the Imperial was one of Chrysler's models. This particular model is a six-passenger Custom Imperial Town limousine with a 133.5-inch wheelbase. This was the first year Chrysler used a one-piece, curved windshield. This was the last year for the extended bellhousing 331-ci block.

Below
Chrysler's first Hemi engine was introduced in 1951. Unfortunately, it was installed in a line of cars with 1940s styling. This Hemi-powered Chrysler New Yorker convertible paced the 1951 Indianapolis 500 race. *DaimlerChrysler Historical Collection*

The rear-seat passenger of the Chrysler Custom Imperial Town Limousine was treated to luxury and comfort. The large bench seat and door panels were covered in a fine wool cloth. Robe rails and chrome handgrips made entry and exit easier. There were footrests on the floor and the divider had a window that would close off the rear passenger compartment from the driver.

goal. It was Exner's job to spearhead the redesign of Chrysler's product line before sales deteriorated further. It wasn't until 1951 that any of Exner's work, albeit minor, could be incorporated into Chrysler's styling. It was also in 1951 that the first Hemi engine was introduced in a Chrysler vehicle.

In 1951, a few of the Chrysler body styles were eliminated from the line. Gone were the six-cylinder Royals and the wood-trimmed Town and Country coupes and convertibles. The basic Chrysler

cars were the same as the 1950 models with a few minor trim changes. The biggest change was the addition of the new Hemi engine available in the Chrysler Saratoga, New Yorker, and Imperial models. With the new V-8, Chrysler could now compete with Cadillac and Oldsmobile on the V-8 playing field. Its only mechanical drawback was the inadequate Fluid Drive automatic transmission. Chrysler was able to showcase its new FirePower Hemi at the 1951 Indianapolis 500, where a New Yorker convertible paced the field. Unfortunately, the new Hemi couldn't correct the dated styling, and Chrysler sales dropped to 11th place overall.

In 1952, one-third of all cars were equipped with a V-8 engine. This was also the first year for the Hemi in the DeSoto. The engine was named FireDome, as was the model of DeSoto in which it was installed. Unfortunately, the 1952 DeSoto's styling was 10 years behind that of the engine. The cowl vent, two-piece flat windshield, and twist-type door handles were all 1930s' era innovations. The only way to distinguish a 1951 DeSoto from a 1950 model was the appearance of a small, functional hood scoop. The FireDome was DeSoto's top-of-the-line model that sold 50,000 units. This pushed DeSoto into 12th place in sales, and dropped Chrysler to 13th. DeSoto's FireDome entry into the 1952 Mobilgas economy run netted 21.27 miles per gallon.

Dodge added Red Ram Hemi power to its new 1953 Coronet. This new Dodge was billed as Chrysler's "Action Car." The new Dodge was also the first to be restyled by Exner and featured softer lines and more glass. One of the most obvious styling changes seen in the restyled Dodge, DeSoto, and Chrysler was a one-piece curved windshield, and one-piece curved rear windows on sedans and hardtops. This replaced the dated two-piece flat windshield and three-piece rear window. All of Chrysler's cars were treated to contemporary interior fabrics, which coordinated with a wide selection of new exterior colors.

Chrysler, Dodge, and DeSoto each had their own version of the Hemi for 1953. While adding complexity and cost, it was also a selling point that each model had its own distinctive engine—something all of the manufacturers were touting at the time. In 1954, Dodge showed that it was the Action Car by pacing the Indy 500 with a Royal 500 convertible that was powered by a 150-horsepower Hemi. Dodge also built 701 replicas that retailed for $2,632. These pace cars featured special side trim, chrome wire wheels, and a continental kit.

The entire Chrysler line of cars was restyled for 1955 with what copywriters described as "the Forward Look." They all received the Exner touch, which included a lower, wider design. The Chrysler, DeSoto, and new Imperial all shared the same basic body. Variations in grilles, taillights, bumpers, and side trim distinguished each line of cars. The most stunning of all was the new

Virgil Exner's superb styling came into full bloom in 1955. Chrysler's redesign of its entire line of cars was said to have cost $100 million to bring to the market. This Chrysler New Yorker convertible rolled on a 126-inch wheelbase and was powered by a 250-horsepower Hemi engine. *DaimlerChrysler Historical Collection*

Chrysler 300C, created by adding an Imperial front end to a Windsor hardtop body. While most cars in 1955 were decorated with an extraordinary amount of chrome, the 300C featured a single chrome strip on the side. With its 300-horsepower Hemi engine, it was America's first muscle car. The 300C made its performance mark at Daytona, where it notched the first three places in the flying mile time trials. Even in 1955, high performance came at a stiff price. The 300C sold for $4,110.

The Imperial was introduced as an entirely new car line in 1955. It was a luxury car designed to compete directly against the

Lincoln and Cadillac. It featured stunning Exner styling, reminiscent of recent Chrysler show cars, and had a Hemi engine. The Imperial featured a split windowpane grille and gun sight taillights. This behemoth rolled on a long, 130-inch wheelbase and had artistic, sculpted circular wheel openings. In keeping with the elegant upscale theme of the car, the two-tone paint schemes restricted the second color to the roof only, unlike the 1955 DeSoto and Dodge triple-tone paint schemes. The new Imperial sold well in 1955 and didn't dip into the sales of the Chrysler car line to do so.

This was also the year that Chrysler and DeSoto dropped their six-cylinder engines and used only V-8 engines. All of Chrysler's cars sold well in 1955 due in large part to the improved styling. Chrysler's strong Hemi V-8s also helped sales, as 78.6 percent of all cars sold in 1955 had a V-8 engine. For the 1955 model year, Dodge placed 8th in sales, Chrysler 9th, DeSoto 12th, and Imperial 17th.

Right
One of the most interesting events in an auto assembly plant is the body drop. It takes several workers to make this happen. Here, a 1955 Chrysler 300C hardtop body is being lowered onto its chassis. The engine, transmission, and exhaust system have already been installed into the frame. The front clip has been laid in position. This is the point where a previously random arrangement of components begins to look like a car. *DaimlerChrysler Historical Collection*

Below
The 1955 Chrysler 300C used an Imperial front clip to distinguish it from other Chrysler models. This particular 300C featured the optional chrome wire wheels. *DaimlerChrysler Historical Collection*

In 1956, DeSoto grew its first set of fins and got rid of its grille teeth. The basic car was an overhauled 1955 model. The fins, albeit tame, were accentuated with a strip of stainless steel that ran the length of the car and abruptly angled up the end of the quarter panel. The taillights went from single small vertical rectangular-shaped lens units to a trio of vertically stacked round lights inset into a notch in the end of the quarter panel. A fine mesh grille with a "V" emblem in the center replaced the teeth. The turn signals were housed in a pair of grille/bumper guards.

Leading the field of 33 contestants to the green flag at Indianapolis in 1956 was a DeSoto FireFlite convertible. The car was white and gold and loaded with every option (including a record turntable) that DeSoto had, except air conditioning. The total weight of this car was 4,490 pounds. *Hot Rod* magazine had a chance to road test this car shortly before the race. A 255-horsepower, 330-ci FireFlite Hemi powered the car. From a standing start, the big DeSoto could reach 60 miles per hour in 9.8 seconds. This time was above average considering the weight of the car. The testers also found the car's stopping power to be excellent,

Exterior high style and interior luxury were the hallmarks of the 1956 Imperial. The interior was a blend of brocade cloth and leather with chrome accents. Imperials ranged in price from $4,500 to $5,000 in 1956.

Left

The Imperial's "gun sight" taillights were positioned onto moderately styled fins in 1956. These lights were one of the most highly identifiable design details of the classy 1956 Imperial.

Above

In 1955, Imperial became a distinct make. The Imperial had always been the most luxurious of all Chrysler models, and it would continue to be so under its own title. This 1956 model had a 133-inch wheelbase, and was powered by a 354-ci Chrysler FirePower V-8 rated at 280 horsepower.

Right

Chrysler's push-button transmission controls debuted in 1956. The PowerFlite transmission did not have a "park" position. When parking the car, the neutral "N" button was selected and the chrome handle for the parking brake, located just below the button panel, was pulled.

because of its 12-inch power-assisted drum brakes. They ran it hard, but the brakes never faded. The editors were disappointed in the lack of feel with power steering, an option required on a car of this weight class. One surprise they noted was the 17.0 miles per gallon it racked up on the highway. The DeSoto's 120-inch wheelbase made for an excellent ride. While pleased with the car's balance (53.5 percent on the front wheels and 46.5 percent on the rear wheels), the testers suggested that the FireFlite borrow some of the heavy-duty chassis components from the DeSoto Adventurer to correct the body roll on turns and the nose-dive on hard braking.

Chrysler's sporty coupe was updated for 1956 and was named the 300-B. The cost of a 300-B was $4,367. It received a new taillight treatment, as did all Chryslers. The big news for the 300-B was the addition of a 355-horsepower engine under the hood. Due to the increased electrical demands of starting a high-compression engine and the addition of electrically powered options, Chrysler, DeSoto, Imperial, and Dodge all moved up to a 12-volt electrical system. This was also the year in which Chrysler's cars would be remembered for their three-tone paint schemes.

The 1956 Dodge also sprouted its first set of modest tail fins on what Dodge called its "Flight Sweep" design. Also introduced in the 1956 Dodge were push-button transmission controls. The best thing that Dodge did in 1956 was to release the D-500 option. It converted a nice V-8–powered street sedan into a performance car.

From the outside, the only indication that this Dodge was more than a pedestrian version of the previous year's model was the presence of a small, crossed checker flag emblem with "500"

Chrysler's advertising department used this 1955 300C to tout its performance capabilities. Exner's new design included these radical tail fins. Within two years, these fins would appear small by comparison. *DaimlerChrysler Historical Collection*

at the base of the flags. These emblems were placed on the front of the hood and on the deck lid. Under the D-500's hood was a 260-horsepower Red Ram Hemi engine. The suspension was beefed up with heavy-duty springs, shocks, and a front sway bar.

Hot Rod magazine tested the Dodge D-500 and wrote the following: "Lovers of high-performance passenger cars can be assured that they can purchase such a car (for about $200 more than a standard Dodge, a ridiculously low price for the quality of the car) and all the necessary equipment to make it equal to a race car in terms of performance, roadability, handling ease, economy of operation, and safety."

Hot Rod magazine tester Racer Brown even took the Dodge D-500 test car to the San Fernando drag strip and won two

The 1956 DeSoto was selected as the Indianapolis 500 pace car. The model used was a limited-edition Adventurer convertible trimmed in white and gold. While this 1956 *Motor Trend* ad features the Indy pace car, it also mentions the balance of the DeSoto line.

Right
This print advertisement for the 1957 Dodge D-500 shows a smiling male driver behind the wheel on a freeway. He's just blown by a slower bus and a Corvette that were in the right lane. The ad raves about the Dodge's 310-horsepower engine and declares, "It talks your language!"

Above
In 1956, the DeSoto lost its trademark toothy grille in favor of a mesh grille. This Sportsman four-door is equipped with optional factory chrome wire wheels.

Right
The DeSoto, like all of Chrysler's other 1956 models, was fitted with new finned quarter panels. The DeSoto's fins were accentuated by a "kick-up" at the end of the body side molding. This was also the first year for the tri-tower taillights.

trophies running the quarter at 83.6 miles per hour. A twin to the test car held the class record at that strip at 84.6 miles per hour. Also available was a D-500 on steroids called as the D-500-1, which included dual quads, and was rated at 295 horsepower. Danny Eames drove a Dodge D-500-1 to a flying mile record of 130 miles per hour at the 1956 Daytona Speedweeks. Dodge sold 240,686 units in 1956, and placed eighth in sales for the year.

All of Chrysler's redesigned offerings for 1957 had big fins. The new Chrysler and sister DeSoto had soaring rear fenders. It was Exner's second generation of the Forward Look and it led the styling parade for 1957. With the release of their restyled line of

The 1956 DeSoto was an elegant car. DeSoto used its distinctive chrome side trim to divide its two-tone paint schemes that were so popular in the mid-1950s.

cars, Chrysler broke with tradition by having two major restyles within three years. The only complaints about the big fins on the 1957 Chrysler products came from new owners who, when they first glanced into the rearview mirror, thought that their car's rear fin was another car alongside their car. Both the Chrysler and DeSoto were equipped with quad headlights, but in several states they were illegal. Single-headlight units were installed on the cars destined for dealerships in those states.

The fins on the new Dodge looked as if they had been bolted to the top of the quarter panel, especially with the two-tone paint scheme. However, this didn't detract from the overall appearance of the car since fins were fashionable in 1957. When fins were first introduced, customers had a hard time getting used to them, but eventually everyone wanted a car with fins.

Up front, the Dodge had an eyebrow over the single head-light, which was accompanied by a large round turn signal. This was in anticipation of the quad headlights to be released on the

To maintain the clean look of the four-door hardtop when the side windows were down, Chrysler's engineers devised this scissors-action window regulator for the rear door windows. No detail was too small when Chrysler's stylists designed the DeSoto. Items as insignificant as the door handles and C-pillar trim received extra attention.

The late 1950s was a time when automotive designers were heavily influenced by the new generation of jet planes. This gave way to smooth bodies and tall tail fins. Some fins looked as though they had been affixed as an afterthought, but the rear fins on the 1957 Chryslers were gracefully blended into the rest of the body. The new Chrysler was longer, lower, and wider than any previous model.

Dodge in 1958. *Motor Trend* magazine tested a new Dodge D-500 in its February 1957 issue. The testers were pleased with the heavy-duty suspension that came with the D-500 option, priced at $72. This was the first year for the torsion bar front suspension.

The D-500 also included a front sway bar and featured stiffer shocks than those on the standard Dodge. This made for a better-handling vehicle than the Buick or Olds it was tested against. The 285-horsepower Red Ram Hemi, backed by a TorqueFlite transmission, powered the test car. It ran the quarter in 17.2 seconds at a speed of 79 miles per hour. These times were equal to or better than the V-8–equipped competition. In 1957, the least expensive Red Ram V-8–equipped Dodge was the Coronet two-door sedan, which was listed for $2,437. The most expensive was the Custom Royal convertible, which sold for $3,091.

Dual exhausts could be added to any V-8 Dodge for an extra $28. They were standard with the D-500 option and the dual-four-barrel Power Pack option. Other options were a TorqueFlite automatic transmission for $220, power windows for $102, and air conditioning for an additional $380. Dodge had finally pulled together a dynamite styling, chassis, transmission, and engine package for 1957. Unfortunately, one of these key components, the Hemi engine, would be eliminated from the 1958 model. Dodge had a great five-year run with its Red Ram Hemis. This would also be the last year for the Hemi in the DeSoto. The handwriting was on the wall.

The March 1957 issue of *Motor Trend* magazine offered an interesting comparison. On pages 10 and 11 was a two-page

spread announcing the new 1957 Chrysler 300C. The double-page photograph featured a shot of a white convertible, top down, blond in the passenger seat, speeding down the beach at Daytona. The advertising copy proclaimed that this was the "newest version of the NASCAR Grand National Champion." It also boldly stated that at 375 horsepower, it was "America's Most Powerful Car."

Flip to page 13 and the headline—in 1-inch font—for Chevrolet's ad reads, "Fuel Injection!" Chevrolet boasted one horsepower per cubic inch with the new fuel injection system in its 283 engine, but the ad's horsepower numbers, weak visual impact, and lack of NASCAR bragging rights fell short of Chrysler's bold ad.

The 1957 300C had the distinction of being the most powerful car on the road, as well as one of the most beautiful. For 1957, it was available in both a hardtop and a convertible. The 300C's overall lines were clean, from its quad headlights to its tall tail fins. While extra chrome was added to DeSotos and other Chrysler models, the 300C was almost completely free of side trim, except for a thin quarter-panel molding that ended in a circular red, white, and blue "300C" emblem.

The grille was trapezoidal in shape and featured a large egg-crate pattern. Rectangular-shaped brake-cooling scoops sat below the headlights. These scoops fed cool air to the front brakes to reduce brake fade. New for 1957 was a SilentFlite fan drive, which limited the fan speed to 2,500 rpm. The standard transmission was a three-speed TorqueFlite automatic with push-button control. A manual transmission was also available. The standard rear-end ratio was 3.36:1, but optional ratios from 2.92:1 down to 6.17:1 were available.

In addition to the 375-horsepower Hemi engine, one of the highlights of the 1957 300C package was its suspension. Like all 1957 Chrysler passenger cars, the 300C rode on front torsion bars. The standard bars were 1.02 inches in diameter, while the heavy-duty 300Cs were 1.11 inches in diameter. This increased the effective spring rate by 40 percent. The rear springs were semi-elliptical leaves that had a 50 percent increase in spring rate over the standard Chrysler rear springs. The wheels on the 300C were 6.5 inches wide and were mounted special Goodyear Blue Streak whitewall tires. At an overall height of 54.7 inches, the 300C had the lowest roofline of all Chrysler products.

The 300C was unique because it was a luxurious family car with unbeatable performance. It only took six years, but Chrysler

When the 1957 Chryslers were introduced, they featured quad headlights. Some states, however, had not yet approved this configuration. Chrysler, therefore, had to build some of these new models with single lamps. The opening below the headlight on this 300C is a brake cooling duct. The inside of the opening is painted red.

Powering the 1957 300C is the 375-horsepower 392-ci Hemi engine. It is topped with dual Carter WCFB four-barrel carburetors.

had finally matched the exterior styling with the speed and technology of the engine and the stability of the chassis. Each owner was warned in the owner's manual to "Respect it for its power, and control its power with care."

At the beginning of 1958, only the Chrysler and the Imperial came with the 392-ci Hemi engine. This would be the last year for the first-generation Hemi engines, since both of these models would be powered by wedge engines in 1959. Chrysler's 1958 model received a mild facelift. Chrysler's designers were smart enough to preserve the signature fins and taillights. They made a change to the front, however, that did not help the overall look of the car. The Hemi departed quietly at the end of 1958. New lighter and more efficient wedge engines were coming off the drawing boards to replace the Hemi.

Chrysler had always been noted for its engineering innovations, and it was the first to offer four-wheel hydraulic brakes, high-compression engines, automatic overdrive transmissions, power-operated convertible tops, full-time power steering, and the Hemi engine. While engineering was flying high, the emphasis on style had been on the back burner since the 1934 Airflow. Virgil Exner stepped in and gave Chrysler's customers the styling to match the engine. The decade of the 1950s was a great one for Chrysler, the Hemi, and automotive history.

The taillight on all 1957 Chryslers used a single large red lens with a smaller backup light below. The 300C emblem on the quarter panel has a background of red, white, and blue.

The interior of all 1957 Chrysler 300Cs was buttery soft tan leather accented in black. The jet-fighter theme was carried to the instrument panel, where two large pods were used for the 150-mile-per-hour speedometer in the left pod, and the engine monitoring gauges in the right pod.

47

CHAPTER THREE

HEMI
B-BODIES

1964–1971

Some times you just never know what kind of name or code may stick for good. In the world of automotive design, a new product receives a code name or letter to identify it until a final model name has been created. These code names often stick and are interchangeable with the product's advertised brand name. Chrysler's midsize passenger car was coded "B-body." That name is still used today among restorers and collectors to identify the 1966–1971 Belvedere, Satellite, Coronet, R/T, and GTX models. (The Road Runner, Super Bee, and 1971 Charger are also B-body cars and are covered later in this book.)

The legacy of the B-body Hemi began in 1964, when a handful of Hemi-equipped Plymouths and Dodges were built for regular consumption. These cars didn't have the acid-dipped body panels or aluminum fenders that the race versions had. There were also no exterior badges to identify the engine. The only giveaway that this car was something out of the ordinary was the massive hood scoop. Unlike the Max Wedge's dual-channel hood scoop, this one was rectangular in shape.

Two different cross-ram–equipped Hemi engines were released in 1964: the high-compression (12.5:1) Holley-equipped version that made its mark on the drag strips, and a lower-compression (11:1)

This modest 1966 Plymouth Belvedere sedan looks like a car a spinster librarian would drive. A closer look at the "426 Hemi" emblems on front fender reveals the beast under the hood. Many Hemi buyers, including the one who originally ordered this car, bypassed the stylish hardtops in favor of lighter-weight, less-expensive sedans for drag racing. ©David Farrell

In 1964, Chrysler released a limited number of the new Hemi engines in Dodge and Plymouth B-bodies that could be driven on the street. These cars had steel bodies and an engine with a lower compression ratio than the race engine. The only indication that this Plymouth Belvedere is Hemi-powered is by the large scoop on the hood. The American mag wheels are an aftermarket addition.

version that used Carter AFB carbs. The lower-compression version was rated at 415 horsepower and the high-compression version at 425. These were the same horsepower ratings attributed to the Max Wedge engines. The exact number of low-compression Hemis sold in 1964 is unknown.

When the 1966 models were introduced, the new Plymouth Belvedere and Dodge Coronet B-bodies looked as though they

had been cut out of a solid block on a milling machine. Every line was angular and sharp corners were abundant. Although the sides were artfully crafted and sculpted in the style of the early 1960s, these clean lines also lagged behind the new styling trends set by General Motors in 1965.

Plymouth and Dodge also had a reputation for designing a standard, boxy sedan. These types of cars were often seen as rental cars or driver training school cars. In the mid-1960s, 34 percent of all police sedans were Plymouths. These weren't the bragging rights the manufacturer was looking for.

Both Dodge and Plymouth were new to the muscle car game. They had produced some of the fastest drag race cars with Max Wedge engines in 1963 and 1964, but these cars were not designed for the street. They also were not packaged as sporty street cruisers.

Above

This 1964 Dodge 440 hardtop is equipped with the 415-horsepower Hemi engine. When this Hemi car was first sold, it was delivered without a factory warranty of any kind. Drag racers preferred the lighter-weight sedans to the hardtops. The small, original-equipment tires (7.50x14) on this Dodge are no match for this high-horsepower engine.

Right

The street version Hemi for 1964 had an 11:1 compression ratio and a pair of Carter AFB carburetors on a cross-ram intake. Race Hemis had a 12.5:1 compression ratio and Holley carbs. All 1964 Hemis had chrome valve covers with "Super Stock 426" decals. The large chrome air cleaner fits within an opening cut into the top of the hood that is covered by the large scoop.

Above

In 1966 Plymouth offered the new street Hemi in the freshly restyled Belvedere B-body. The front end featured a grille with thin horizontal bars and two large parking lights. This is one of the 531 Belvedere II hardtops equipped with a Hemi engine. All 1966 Hemi cars came with Goodyear Blue Streak tires.

Right

The simple bench-seat interior of the 1966 Belvedere was strictly utilitarian. The long handle of the Inland-manufactured, four-speed shifter emerges through the floor in a large rubber boot. The Hurst shifter would not become standard equipment on Hemi cars for several years.

The top-of-the-line Plymouth B-body in 1966 was the Satellite. It had the same body as the Belvedere, but instead of a wide side molding, it featured a slender beltline molding, thin wheel opening moldings, and bright rocker panel strips. The chrome road wheels on this Satellite were not original components in 1966. This car was originally equipped with full wheel covers and Blue Streak tires.

They just happened to be inexpensive, lightweight sedans with engines that rocked.

Chrysler's first attempt at a muscle car designed for the street was the Hemi-powered 1966 B-body. Unfortunately, the exterior body styling looked too much like the pedestrian sedans that spinster schoolteachers and librarians were buying at the time. What these cars lacked in muscle car style, they made up for in the brawn of their engine.

The Belvedere and Coronet were built on the same platform, but the Coronet had a wheelbase 1 inch longer than the Belvedere's 116 inches. This also translated into a longer overall length at 203 inches for the Coronet, versus 200.5 inches for the Belvedere. The base price for a Belvedere hardtop was $2,412, while the Dodge Coronet 440 hardtop listed for $2,439; the upscale 500 listed for $2,592.

The Hemi engine was available in three Belvedere models (Belvedere I, Belvedere II, and Satellite) and four Coronet models (Coronet, Coronet Deluxe, Coronet 440, and Coronet 500). Curb '

weight for the base Belvedere was 3,200 pounds, and the Dodge weighed 3,395 pounds. Hemi-equipped B-bodies received a heavy-duty suspension that included larger, 11-inch brakes and 7.75x14-inch tires on 5.5-inch-wide wheels. Disc brakes were optional at $41.45 and required power assist. Even though the Hemi received the larger police-package drum brakes, they were the weakest link in a very stout package.

Motor Trend was one of the first magazines to road test the Hemi-equipped 1966 Plymouth Satellite. The Satellite was the up-graded sporty version of the Belvedere. It had bucket seats, a console, and special exterior trim. The base price for a 1966 Satellite was $2,695. The car that *Motor Trend* tested listed for $4,211, and included the $900 Hemi option.

The only visible exterior items that differentiated the Hemi-equipped Satellite from one with a smaller engine (other than the gun sight hood ornament with the numbers "4-2-6" stacked verti-cally) were the small Hemi emblems on the front fender and the 7.75x14-inch Goodyear blue-streak tires. There were no special wheels, hood scoops, or racing stripes.

It took a brave soul in 1966 to lay down an extra grand for a Hemi engine, especially when the base price of a Corvette convertible was only $4,084 and a 425-horsepower 427-ci engine could be added for only $312. Then again, it was only a Corvette, and not a Hemi.

The taillights and bumpers were the same on all 1966 Plymouth B-body Belvederes and Satellites. The rear deck trim on the Satellite was subdued with black insets. Nestled cleanly into that deck trim were the backup lights, a federally mandated safety item in 1966. To the side of the "Satellite" script on the right side of the deck lid is a small red, white, and blue emblem used only on the Satellite.

As Plymouth's premier B-body in 1966, the Satellite featured an upgraded interior with bucket seats, chrome console, and standard floor shift for the TorqueFlite. The vinyl covering on the seats featured thin vertical pleats bordered with two narrow panels that resembled hand-tooled leather. The steering wheel cover is an aftermarket item. Hidden by the steering wheel is the console-mounted tachometer.

Motor Trend's objective was to see if the new Hemi was tame enough to be driven on the streets. Their driving course led from Detroit to Los Angeles via New Orleans—a 4,000-mile trip on all kinds of street surfaces. With the Satellite's 3.23 final gearing, *Motor Trend*'s drivers could maintain a cruising speed of 80 miles per hour with an engine speed of 3,500 rpm. This kept them well out of the range of the second four-barrel. The drivers complained about the small size of the gas tank (19 gallons) and the fact they had to stop every 170 miles to fill it up. Each refueling stop along the way, however, became a learning experience for the station's attendants and curious observers who wanted to know more about the Hemi.

Motor Trend's drivers were impressed by the Satellite's road manners and handling, made possible by the heavy-duty police suspension components that were standard on the Hemi. *Motor Trend*'s biggest complaint was directed at the clunky four-speed shift mechanism. They ran two tests at the strip, the first with the stock Inland shifter. The Satellite ran the quarter in 15.0 seconds at 94 miles per hour. When they added a Hurst shifter, it ran 14.5 at 99 miles per hour. Unfortunately, gearing and tires were factory specified, which limited the Satellite's ultimate potential.

Chrysler was quick to learn that loaning a journalist a high-performance car to drive reaped big benefits. One article in a magazine was worth thousands of dollars in print advertising. *Car Life* magazine was the next to receive a 1966 Hemi-powered Satellite to test. It was almost identical to the one *Motor Trend* drove, except it was equipped with TorqueFlite. *Car Life* also found the Hemi, when cautiously driven, to be "docile, tractable, and not the least brutish." They also found that full-throttle runs produced excessive wheel spin.

Similar to the *Motor Trend* test car, *Car Life*'s Hemi also got poor mileage (11.1 miles per gallon) during their test. One of the

The Belvedere II lacked the snappy styling of other 1966 muscle cars, such as the GTO or Chevelle SS 396. The Belvedere II did offer one option that no one else could—the Hemi. Only 10 Belvedere II convertibles were equipped with the Hemi engine in 1966.

most interesting photos of the Satellite tested by *Car Life* was a shot of it pulling out of a gas station with the sign in the background reading, "Chevron Supreme, 35.9." At that price, you could fill the Satellite's 19-gallon tank for only $6.82. In comparison, a 1966 Satellite with a 383 engine registered a paltry 13.4 miles per gallon in a March 1966 *Car Life* road test.

Plymouth didn't waste any time promoting the new Hemi Satellite. In the March 1966 issue of *Car Life* magazine, it bought an eight-page color center spread that featured page after page of Hemi successes and coverage of the new street Hemi. On the second and third pages, all of Hemi's important specifications were listed with a double-page photo of a bright red Satellite hardtop at speed. The ad's copywriters filled the text with comparisons to the race Hemis and how the engine had evolved for street use. The ad also included four pages of color photos and performance numbers of Hemi-powered race cars. The final page of the ad was a contest entry form that gave the reader

the chance to win a new Hemi-powered Satellite. All the reader had to do was guess the total elapsed running time and the average winning speed of a Hemi Satellite at the March 27, 1966, Atlanta 500.

Years later, Tom Hoover, Chrysler's "Father of the Hemi," admitted that the solid-lifter dual quad Hemi may have been more than the average automotive enthusiast could chew in one bite. In hindsight, he said that it might have been more practical to release a single-quad hydraulic-lifter street version. A Hemi in that configuration, at a slightly lower price, may have had wider appeal. Then again, there can only be one king at the top of the hill.

With the 1967 model year, B-body Dodges and Plymouths received only minor changes to the exterior and interior. The biggest change was the way the cars were packaged. Stripes, wheels, and scoops vaulted the spinster sedans into the go-go-boot world of the muscle car.

Dodge selected the R/T (Road/Track) as its premiere muscle car and Plymouth chose the GTX. The GTX handle came about because Jack Smith, Plymouth's chief product planning manager, wanted something that "sounded like GTO." Catchy names were part of the marketing game that turned a high-horsepower sedan into a highly identifiable muscle car.

The Hemi B-body could always hold its own in a horsepower battle, but now it had the performance look that equaled the

THE SILVER BULLET—
THE ULTIMATE
HEMI STREET RACER

Jimmy Addison was one of the most feared street racers in the Detroit area. He drove a heavily modified Hemi-powered 1967 GTX that was silver in color and earned the name *The Silver Bullet* by consistently being the fastest on the street. ©*Dale Amy*

To many Detroiters, Jimmy Addison is as big a local hero as Detroit Tiger Al Kaline, or Detroit Red Wing Gordie Howe. Addison is the street racer who built and raced the baddest Hemi-powered street racer of all time—*The Silver Bullet*.

The Silver Bullet started its life as a standard 1967 Plymouth Belvedere GTX. It was originally a Chrysler test car assigned to an engineering group that experimented with different component combinations on the 440 engine. Following its service at Chrysler, the car fell into the hands of Jimmy Addison. Addison had gained a worthy reputation for tuning cars and street racing with his 1962 Max Wedge Dodge. He also managed a Sunoco gas station on Woodward Avenue—the epicenter of Detroit's street racing scene. Addison converted the car to Hemi power. He had a connection at Chrysler who was able to procure some of the finest specialized lightweight components and Hemi parts available at the time.

The Silver Bullet's Hemi engine was bored and stroked for a total displacement of 487 cubic inches. Beneath the aluminum heads was a set of 12:1 pistons. The cam was a Racer Brown with 0.590 lift and 322 degrees of duration. The magnesium cross-ram intake was fitted with two Holley 780-cfm carburetors. The engine was estimated to produce 600 horsepower. Backing the engine was a TorqueFlite transmission with a 4,000-rpm stall converter. The rear-end ratios were either 4:30 or 4:56. Twelve-inch-wide M&H slicks were run on the street and strip.

The body was fitted with fiberglass fenders, doors, hood, and deck lid. In total, 500 pounds were removed from the Belvedere's weight. The quarter panels were flared slightly by cutting several vertical slits in the sheet metal and pulling the pieces out far enough

to allow the wide slicks to slip in. Then the strips were welded together and smoothed over.

Gary Jankowski was a Woodward regular and remembers seeing *The Silver Bullet* parked at the Sunoco station on Woodward. "I never saw Addison race on the street, but I do remember seeing him pull into Howard Johnson's where members of the High End Club [a Detroit street racers club] hung out. That car crouched like a cat with the headers dragging on the ground as he came in the driveway. Once in the lot, Addison winged the engine and pulled a hole shot." Jankowski remembers seeing *The Silver Bullet* run at Detroit Dragway. "He was running mid-10s at close to 140 miles per hour. Addison ran through the mufflers and it was whisper quiet through the traps."

The legend of *The Silver Bullet* was further enhanced when it was featured in the September 1971 issue of *Car Craft* magazine. It was there that author Ro McGonegal dubbed this factory street racer the "Silver Bullet." Today the car no longer races, but has been lovingly restored by Hemi collector Harold Sullivan.

muscle under the hood. The GTX and R/T were both designed to be loaded with standard performance options. The base engine was the 440-ci Magnum V-8 rated at 375 horsepower and backed by a standard TorqueFlite automatic transmission with a four-speed optional at no extra cost.

A dual-snorkel air cleaner and chrome valve covers dressed the engine. On the inside, vinyl-covered bucket seats, a chrome console, and a floor shift were standard options. A heavy-duty suspension with chrome exhaust tips, 11-inch drum brakes, and

7.75x14-inch red-line tires rounded out the package. Power disc brakes were optional. The GTX had a small pair of nonfunctional hood scoops and a "pit-stop" gas cap (a flip-top racing cap) on the left quarter.

The R/T's hood had three large nonfunctional louvers in the center and a unique grille with thin vertical bars similar to the one on the Dodge Charger. Both cars had chrome road wheels as an option, and the GTX had an optional set of hood and deck stripes. The GTX and R/T were well-rounded muscle cars with a

The Coronet was Dodge's B-body car in 1966. It shared the same basic body structure as the Belvedere, but had revised quarter panels and a different front clip. This Coronet Deluxe two-door sedan was a former race car and is one of 49 built in 1966 with the Hemi engine. Like all Hemi cars in 1966, it came with Goodyear Blue Streak tires.

potent standard engine and a long list of standard, heavy-duty engine and chassis components.

The only optional engine on the 1967 Plymouth GTX and Dodge R/T was the Hemi. When the option was ordered, small "Hemi" emblems were placed on the lower corner of the front fenders on the GTX. The R/T used "426 Hemi" emblems that were placed on the sides of the front fenders.

In addition to the 1967 Dodge R/T and Plymouth GTX, Hemi-hungry customers were able to order their favorite 425-horsepower engine in a variety of standard Belvederes and Coronets, including a model built expressly for NHRA SS/B competition (see chapter 8).

There were only 108 Hemi-optioned GTXs and 61 Dodge R/Ts in 1967. Total Hemi production for all 1967 B-bodies amounted to 316. There were 119 Dodges and 197 Plymouths sold with the Hemi engine—less than half the number sold in 1966. The new GTX and R/T packages were well engineered and reasonably priced: each had a sticker price of less than $3,200. Sales of 1967 models were slug-gish due in part to the outdated body style. The less expensive, but muscular, 440 engine hurt Hemi sales.

In 1968, Mopar buyers finally got what they were looking for—a stylish new body. The rectilinear lines and sharp corners of the past two years were gone. The new GTX and R/T would be based on a smoothly styled body that was the equal of its contemporaries in the muscle car market.

The GTX and R/T models would both continue as Chrysler's upscale muscle cars and the new Road Runner and Super Bee were the stripped-down street fighters. In 1968, all high-performance engines were limited to these four models and the freshly restyled Dodge Charger.

A 1968 Plymouth GTX hardtop was priced at $3,355. That was $321 more than the base Road Runner hardtop. A convertible was available in GTX trim in 1968, but not as a Road Runner.

The GTX came standard with all the trim that the Road Runner lacked. The interior trim level was higher, with additional brightwork and standard bucket seats. A center console and power windows were also available on the GTX. The exterior performance image was confirmed with the use of the Road Runner's simulated side-vent hood and a set of lower door stripes that ended in front of the rear wheel near a large "GTX" emblem. Like the Road Runner, red-stripe tires were standard and chrome Road Wheels were available, except on the Hemi, where 15-inch wheels were required. The Hemi engine option on the 1968 GTX cost $604.75, and only 410 hardtops and 36 convertibles were equipped with this option.

The 1968 Dodge R/T was the Super Bee's big brother. It offered all of the upscale trim and luxury options that were lacking on the

Above

With the release of the GTX option in 1967, Plymouth moved up a notch in the muscle car appearance department. Red-line tires were standard, and the new chrome Road Wheels were optional. Also standard on the GTX were nonfunctional twin hood scoops and a flip-top fuel cap. A flat black hood and deck stripes were also optional, but are not featured on this particular 1967 GTX. Only 108 1967 GTXs were sold with the Hemi engine.

Right

In 1967, Plymouth went to quad headlights and used the same basic grille as in 1966. The inboard light replaced the turn-signal light that moved down into the bumper.

Below

In 1967, Dodge introduced its R/T option for the Coronet. It featured a unique grille that was similar to the one on the Dodge Charger (but without the retractable headlights) and a hood with simulated louvers. The standard engine was the 375-horsepower 440 Magnum. The Hemi was optional for $564. This is one of only two Hemi R/T convertibles built in 1967.

In 1968, the GTX was Plymouth's top-of-the-line B-body. It featured standard bucket seats and a 440 engine. Also standard on the GTX was a pair of body side stripes that ran along the lower door and ended on the quarter panel with a large chrome "GTX" emblem. As noted by the license plate, this 1968 GTX convertible is one of 36 equipped with a Hemi engine

The 1968 Plymouth GTX used the same hood as the Road Runner. When the GTX was equipped with a Hemi engine, "Hemi" was spelled out on the side vent inserts.

Super Bee. The R/T also came standard with the 375-horsepower 440-ci engine. It shared its Power Dome hood with the Super Bee and had standard side stripes and optional Bumblebee stripes. Hemi production numbers for the 1968 Dodge R/T's were 220 hardtops and 9 convertibles.

The 1969 Plymouth GTX and the 1969 Dodge Coronet R/T both received very few changes from their 1968 versions. New and standard with the Hemi engine on both cars was a cold-air induction package called Ram Charger on the R/T, and Air Grabber on the GTX. This system required an elaborate underhood air duct that sealed to the air cleaner when the hood was closed. These ducts opened to a pair of small hood scoops (on the R/T) or to the twin vertical hood vents (on the GTX). On the side of each hood intake, the name "Hemi" was spelled out in small chrome letters.

The 1969 Dodge Coronet R/T, when equipped with a Hemi, was fitted with a Ramcharger fresh-air system. This system consisted of a pair of hood scoops that connected to underhood ducting. When optioned with a Hemi engine, the outside of each scoop featured a small "Hemi" emblem. The Ramcharger hood was also available as an option with other four-barrel–equipped engines.

Above
Side scoops, an option on the 1969 Dodge Coronet R/T, were mounted on the quarter panel and cost the buyer an extra $35.80.

Above
This 1969 Dodge Coronet R/T convertible is one of 10 built with a Hemi engine. Unlike the GTX and Road Runner convertible, the Coronet R/T was the only performance Dodge convertible available in 1969.

Left

The rear of the 1969 Coronet R/T featured three taillights that were very similar in design to those on the Dodge Charger. The wide Bumblebee stripe is bordered by two thinner stripes. These stripes were standard and came in white, red, and black. When the stripes were deleted, a chrome "R/T" emblem was placed on the quarter panel.

These fresh-air systems were available as an option on both the GTX and R/T with the 440 engine.

Unique to each car was a new set of stripes. The R/T had an additional set of optional scoops for the quarter panels. Ninety-seven Dodge R/T hardtops and 10 convertibles were equipped with a Hemi in 1969. Plymouth sold 198 GTX hardtops and 11 convertibles with the Hemi engine.

Both the GTX and Dodge Coronet R/T were restyled from the beltline down for 1970. The most dramatic change was in the front end of the Dodge. The new grille had a wide center split. The twin openings were horse collar–shaped and surrounded with a halo-style bumper. The look was unique. If two large eyes had been set into the openings instead of its quad headlights, it would have made the perfect face for a Muppet. The rear of the Dodge R/T, however, was nicely styled and featured a blackout panel with three lights on each side.

This assembly-line photo shows how a 1969 Coronet body was dropped down over the engine and K-member assembly. The narrower wedge engines, such as the one in the photo, made the job easier than the wide Hemi. The large piece of paper on the front of the car is a build sheet that defines for the assemblers with which options this car will be built. *DaimlerChrysler Archives*

Below
For 1970, Dodge redesigned the front of the Coronet. The twin horse collar–shaped grilles were greeted with mixed reviews. The side scoops returned on the R/T with a single quarter-panel scoop instead of the twin scoops used on the 1969 R/Ts. This was the only 1970 Coronet R/T convertible produced with a Hemi engine.

Other features on the R/T included revised quarter-panel scoops and standard Bumblebee stripes. Sales of the 1970 Dodge R/T were weak, with only 2,408 units sold. Of those vehicles, only 14 were Hemi-powered. This would be the last year for the Dodge Coronet R/T.

Unlike the 1970 Coronet, the Plymouth GTX was only available as a hardtop. The new GTX models were also restyled with a redesign that was slightly more mainstream than its Coronet brother. New quarter panels, a new taillight treatment, and front-end sheet metal were added for a fresh appearance. The quarter panels were more rounded and featured a small, nonfunctional rear brake scoop behind the door opening. Standard side stripes, available in white, black, or gold, accented the scoop.

The GTX also shared its Power Dome hood with the Road Runner. As was the case with the Road Runner, the hood could be painted with special black trim stripes, listed as the Performance Hood Paint option. The only engine identification on the GTX was on the back of the hood's Power Dome. The new Air Grabber was standard on the Hemi-equipped GTXs. From behind the wheel, the driver could flip a vacuum switch that would open the trap door–style Air Grabber scoop. This allowed cool air to flow into the engine and exposed the creative graphics on the side of the scoop. For those who settled for one of the two 440-ci engines, the Air Grabber was a $65.55 addition that was worth every penny.

In the previous two years, 15-inch wheels were required with the Hemi engine. In 1970, the Hemi-equipped GTX was no longer required to run the 15-inch wheels, and all Hemis came standard with 14x6-inch wheels. The 15-inch Rallye wheels that mounted F60-15 Goodyear Polyglas white-letter tires were now an option. Of the 7,202 GTX sales in 1970, only 72 were Hemi-equipped.

In 1971, the Coronet name was dropped and all Dodge B-body models were called Chargers. The performance models were the Charger R/T and the Super Bee, which was a car line of its own based on the Charger. Plymouth's B-body was now named the Satellite Sebring. Both new models shared the same 115-inch platform, although the Plymouth body was 2.2 inches shorter. Only a hardtop would be offered in the new B-body. Sales of convertibles had been on a constant decline and the government was threatening added legislation for rollover protection. All manufacturers were deleting convertible models in the early 1970s. The two performance models of the Satellite Sebring were the Road Runner and the GTX.

The new B-body for 1971 was a vast departure from the previous B-body styling. It was smoother, more rounded, and looked larger than its predecessor. The hood was long and the rear edge concealed the hidden windshield wipers. The front end featured a halo-style bumper that could be specified with a body-color Endura coating.

The GTX's wheel openings were slightly flared and accented the car's wide track. With the Hemi engine, the trap-door Air Grabber hood was standard. In 1971, performance cars took a big hit from insurance providers. The GTX was one of the cars squarely in the sights of the underwriters. This fact was confirmed when only 35 Hemi-powered GTXs were sold in 1971.

Throughout the mid- and late 1960s, the Chrysler B-bodies anchored the entire Dodge and Plymouth lineup. While not always on the leading edge of styling, they offered a solid car at a reasonable price. What they were able to offer better than anyone else was two of the best performance engines of the era—the 440 and the Hemi. Chrysler's engineers were smart enough to combine these engines with bulletproof transmission, rear end, and chassis packages. While not as flashy as the sporty 'Cudas and Challengers, the dependable B-body could hold its own in a quick side-by-side street race or on the strip.

The 1970 Plymouth GTX used the new body side scoops to its best advantage by having the twin side stripes disappear into the opening. On the inside were new high-back bucket seats and a woodgrain-trimmed instrument panel with a Rallye cluster. *DaimlerChrysler Archives*

The entire Plymouth line was redesigned for 1971. The new Plymouth GTX was much more rounded than the previous model. The wheel openings were slightly flared and trimmed with a thin chrome molding. "Hemi" was spelled out boldly on the hood's side-facing scoops. The GTX featured this unique transverse hood stripe. *DaimlerChrysler Archives*

HEMI ROAD RUNNERS AND SUPER BEES

1968–1971

In the mid-1960s, Chrysler's muscle cars suffered from an identity crisis. While it offered big engines and finely tuned powertrains, its cars lacked a certain distinctive machismo. Pontiac's GTO, Chevy's SS 396, Olds' 442, and Ford's Fairlane GT all had a muscle-bound load of charisma, along with stout powerplants. A serious makeover was needed.

Chrysler product planner Joe Strum was presented with the nucleus of an idea by the sales team. It was their thought to build a stripped-down car with the biggest engine possible as standard equipment. Their initial definition of "stripped down" meant no rear seat or any ornamentation whatsoever. Strum knew that this kind of bare-bones car would appeal only to a small segment of the market. As a product planner, he knew how to slice, dice, and dissect the market. He plotted the types of people who bought muscle cars, the options they preferred, and the amount of performance they desired.

One of the magic numbers that continued to emerge was the car's ability to reach 100 miles per hour in the quarter mile. That speed was the Rosetta stone that everyone looked to for legitimate straight-line performance.

The 1970 Road Runner was the last model based on the original B-body design that was first released in 1968. Over its short life, the Road Runner was given yearly improvements without losing its original muscle car character. This hardtop is one of 135 hardtops built with the Hemi engine in 1970.

HEMI ROAD RUNNER: 0-105 IN 13.5 SECS.! ONE OF THE REASONS MOTOR TREND NAMED IT...

CAR OF THE YEAR

See facts, figures, NHRA acceleration times—Page 127

Plymouth's 1968 Road Runner received a major boost when *Motor Trend* magazine selected it as its "Car of the Year" in 1968. The new Road Runner provided a swaggering muscle car image and a potent standard 383 V-8 (with optional Hemi) at a low price.

Right
When the Road Runner was initially introduced, it was only available as a two-door coupe. Later in the 1968 model run, a hardtop was introduced. In 1969, a convertible was released. The side view of this 1969 Road Runner hardtop highlights the clean styling that attracted buyers.

had to have the sexy appeal of the established muscle cars. The styling of the 1966 and 1967 Plymouth Belvedere and GTX models was out of step with their contemporaries. These models were boxy and featured sculpted sides—a styling trend of the early 1960s. The muscle cars of the mid-1960s had smoothly rounded bodies with either a scoop that could be made functional or some sort of twin hood grilles.

Good fortune smiled upon the Road Runner product planners in the form of the scheduled redesign of the Belvedere. The Road Runner now had a smoothly rounded body that it shared with the base Belvedere and the upscale GTX. A styling feature that designers had long awaited was curved side glass. It was used to its best advantage in Chrysler's 1968 offerings and contributed to the overall rounded shape of the new Road Runner.

The Road Runner's grille was the same egg-crate design as the standard Belvedere, but it was accented in black. The Road Runner used the same hood as the GTX, with its side-facing, nonfunctional vents. The wheelbase for the 1968 models

The second consideration was price. Strum noted that quarter-mile performance came at a price. The more money someone spent, the faster they could go: any car capable of 100-miles-per-hour speeds cost in excess of $3,300. His goal was to build this speed factor into a $3,000 car.

The result of the product planning group's calculations was the 1968 Road Runner and the slightly higher-priced spin-off, the 1968 Dodge Super Bee. With the high-performance version of the 383 as the base engine—and a price of $2,896—the new Road Runner would stop the timers at the end of the quarter at 100 miles per hour. To prove it to everyone, Plymouth brought in drag racer Ronnie Sox and gave him a new Road Runner to test. He zipped down Irwindale's quarter mile with an elapsed time of 14.01 seconds at a speed of 101.80 miles per hour. To prove that it didn't take a professional driver to reach those numbers, a Chrysler employee got behind the wheel and ran the quarter at 100.22 miles per hour. Mission accomplished!

Chrysler also knew that it would take more than a low price and quick times at the drag strip to sell the new Road Runner. It

Dodge brought its muscle-bound Super Bee into the 1968 Muscle Car wars. It featured many of the key components of the 1968 Road Runner, including the 383-ci, 335-horsepower engine and its stripped-down street racer approach to the market. There were 125 Hemi-equipped Super Bees in 1968. *DaimlerChrysler Historical Collection*

When the new Road Runner was released in 1968, the B-body heritage from 1967 was nowhere to be seen. The body was smoothly rounded and every bit as good looking as any of the established muscle cars of the day.

remained at 116 inches, but the front and rear track width was increased by one-half inch. While the GTX came with stylish bucket seats and carpeted floors, the new Road Runner only had a bench seat and a rubber floor mat.

The 1968 Road Runner's real beauty was in its simplicity. It looked as docile as a senior citizen's sedan. Initially, the Road Runner was introduced as a pillared coupe. Later in the 1968 model year, a hardtop version was available. Convertible Road Runners were never produced in 1968.

Exterior trim on the new Road Runner was minimal and discreet. At the front edge of the door was a small chrome plate

that announced this was a Road Runner. Just to the rear of that emblem was a small decal of the cunning little bird at full cartoon-speed. The deck lid featured a small standing version of the bird. Later in the model year, a decor group was added that featured the bird at speed, followed by a column of dust. Hubcaps were limited to the small, dog-dish models. When the Hemi engine was specified, the standard 14-inch-diameter wheels were replaced with 15-inch, F-70 Polyglas tires.

The Hemi was the only optional engine for the 1968 Road Runner. If the fifth digit on a 1968 Road Runner's serial number was a "J," it was equipped with a 426-ci, 425-horsepower Hemi engine. When equipped with a Hemi, the appliqué on the simulated hood vent spelled out "HEMI." The Hemi engine came standard with a four-speed transmission, but the TorqueFlite automatic was a no-cost option.

The Performance Axle Package, which included the Dana Sure-Grip rear axle, was required with the Hemi. Along with the Hemi engine option came a larger radiator and power front disc brakes.

The rear deck panel on the 1970 Road Runner had a shape similar to the grille. The stripes across the rear were standard on the hardtops and convertibles and optional on coupes. All Road Runners were equipped with dual exhaust systems. California Hemi cars received special mufflers that were quieter than those on Hemi cars manufactured for the other 49 states.

In 1968, 1,011 customers selected option code 23 for the Hemi engine. They were the ones who paid the extra $714 for the privilege and honor of owning a piece of history. Because of the late introduction of the hardtop, only 171 were built, versus 840 coupes.

Unfortunately, the introduction of the 1968 Super Bee in February 1968 was lost in the swirling cloud of excitement that encircled the sexy new Dodge Charger. Like the 1968 Road Runner, the Super Bee was intended to be Dodge's version of a low-cost, stripped-down muscle car. It featured the same high-performance 383 engine as the Road Runner, and the only optional engine was the Hemi. Priced at $714, the Hemi came standard with the four-speed, but the TorqueFlite was a no-cost alternative. Only 125 1968 Super Bees were equipped with the Hemi engine: 94 with the TorqueFlite, and 31 with the four-speed. None of the 1968 Super Bees had exterior engine badges. This made street racing interesting for those who decided to take on a 1968 Super Bee at a stoplight because only the owner knew whether the car had the fast 383 or the very fast Hemi.

Right
The Air Grabber hood was new for 1970 and came standard with the Hemi engine. It featured a vacuum-actuated trapdoor in the center of the hood. When the Air Grabber was open, cool outside air flowed to the air filter below. The sides of the Air Grabber were trimmed with highly creative graphics.

Above
While the doors and roof remained the same, the balance of the sheet metal on the 1970 Road Runner was changed. It was available in coupe, hardtop, and convertible body styles. The 1970 GTX was limited to a hardtop only. This would be the third and last year for the first-generation Road Runner body.

Left
The rear of the Power Bulge hood was the location for the 1970 Road Runner's only engine call-out. Turn-signal indicators were located on each side of the "Hemi" emblem.

In 1968, the Super Bee was available only in the coupe model, which had quarter windows that were hinged at the front, allowing them to swing out at the rear. Giving the Super Bee its exceptional look was the same Power Bulge hood found on the Dodge R/T, as well as the distinctive pair of Bumblebee stripes that wrapped over the rear of the car. On each side, within the stripes, was the circular Super Bee logo. These stripes came in black or white, depending on the color of the car.

The 1968 Road Runner's bench-seat interior was initially offered in blue, parchment, or black and silver. When the Decor Group was introduced in 1968, and the two-door hardtop was available in Road Runner trim, several other colors were added. From the start, the 1968 Super Bee offered a wide choice of interior trim combinations.

Bucket seats were not a Road Runner or Super Bee option in 1968. Even without bucket seats, the option list was long and customers surprised Chrysler's marketing staff by loading the new Road Runners and Super Bees with extras. A tachometer was

Above
The standard interior on a 1970 Road Runner included an all-vinyl bench seat. Bucket seats and a console were optional. This Hemi Road Runner had a four-speed transmission that included a sturdy Hurst "pistol-grip" shifter.

Right
The sides of the 1970 Road Runner were free of any extra trim or chrome. The little cartoon bird was featured on the front fender of the 1970 Road Runner, and a small "Road Runner" emblem was placed on the nonfunctional quarter-panel scoop. These 14-inch styled Road Wheels were an option available with the Hemi engine. *DaimlerChrysler Historical Collection*

In 1971, Dodge dropped the Coronet name and the Super Bee became a Charger model. The new body featured hidden windshield wipers and flush door handles. Bumblebee stripes were no longer part of the Super Bee package, but new side stripes that wrapped around the cowl were standard. Also included were hood graphics with a circular Super Bee logo. These stripes came only in black (even on black cars) and could be deleted.

available for $48.17, front disc brakes for $72.95 (which required the power brake option at $41.75), and the Performance Hood Treatment ($18.05), which added a blacked-out panel to the top of the hood.

Chrysler's low-cost muscle car experiment was a success, and in 1969 both cars became even better. A Super Bee hardtop model was offered in 1969 and the Road Runner added a convertible. In addition, a longer list of sporty options was added. Road Runner buyers also saw a $300 decrease in price for the base coupe. It was a very good year for the Road Runner.

For the 1969 model year, the Road Runner's body remained unchanged, with only minor alterations made to the grille and taillights. The hood was also new and featured a pair of vertical vents. When the Hemi engine was installed, these vents were

Right inset
Hemi-equipped Super Bees were fitted with a standard Ramcharger hood scoop. A vacuum switch under the driver's side of the instrument panel controlled this door.

Below
The stylish Coke-bottle shape of the 1971 Super Bee's side and the severely tucked-under lower body can be seen in this front view. Color-keyed bumpers were available in five colors in 1971, but not in the Butterscotch color of this 1971 Super Bee. Hood pins were optional.

The 1971 Super Bee's side stripe accentuates its smoothly curved quarter panels. The all-black vinyl top, chrome mirrors, and rear spoiler were optional. There were 22 Hemi-equipped Super Bees built in 1971.

The 1971 Super Bee came with a rather plain, all-vinyl bench seat interior. Bucket seats and a console were optional. This car does have the Tuff steering wheel option, which was only available with a TorqueFlite transmission.

connected to the Air Grabber's fresh-air, underhood ducting that provided cooler, outside air to the engine's carburetors. The grilles for this system were either black or red. Red grilles were only used with the optional black hood paint.

On the sides of the hood's vertical vents were the engine designations of either 383 or Hemi. The Air Grabber hood was available as an option with the base 383 engine. Power windows, center console, and bucket seats were added to the option list on both the Road Runner and Super Bee. This brought both cars in line with the comfort and convenience options available on GTOs and SS 396 Chevelles.

The three, two-barrel carburetor-equipped, 390-horsepower, 440-ci engine was added as a midyear option to the 1969 Road Runner option list. Dubbed the "440 Six-Pack," this engine came with three Holley two-barrel carburetors.

Its hood was made of fiberglass, featured a big scoop emblazoned with "440 6BL," and was anchored with four racing-style pins. It was equipped with the usual Hemi heavy-duty chassis and

DRIVING A HEMI ROAD RUNNER

Working for a living is tough. Some guys get to sit in a cubicle all day, and some guys get to drive a Hemi Road Runner and write about it. The sound and feel of the engine's dual quads opening was something I'll never forget.

My friend, Akbar Ali, flipped me the key to his perfectly restored 1969 Hemi Road Runner and said, "You drive." At first I just stared at the key, knowing that this little silver piece of metal was something that thousands of gearheads would like to have in their hands. As I opened the door and slipped behind the wheel, I fought to suppress the big grin that was about to explode on my face. I tried to be as cool as I could and stifle the "YEEHAWWWW" that I wanted to yell.

The seat was more comfortable than I had imagined. I like a car with ample legroom, and the Road Runner's bucket seat was perfectly placed for me.

I slipped the key into the ignition switch and gave it a little turn to the right, and the engine sprang to life with a clatter. I winged the throttle twice to get a feel for the pedal, and because I wanted to hear the engine. Just before dropping the TorqueFlite into gear, I was warned to watch the handling with the bias-ply tires. As I drove through city streets, I was surprised at how docile and controllable the Hemi engine seemed to be. Its brutish power stayed well within rein as I drove through stop-and-go traffic on my way to the freeway. One of the first things I did was turn off the radio so I could listen to the engine. I also noticed how the sheet metal on the hood vibrated while idling at a stoplight. The transmission shifted beautifully as I accelerated onto the freeway. The 4.10 gears made for a noisy 3,500-rpm engine speed to keep up with traffic, and were a bit stiff for extended freeway driving.

To limit engine speed, I kept to the slower lanes on the right. Soon, I noticed a lowered, late-model Honda to my left. I looked over and saw three guys in their late teens or early 20s in the car.

The dude in the passenger seat rolled down the window and asked, "What year?" I yelled back, "A '69." Upon my answer, the guy in the back seat of the Honda pumped his fist as if he had just scored the winning touchdown in the Super Bowl. Great cars transcend all kinds of generational boundaries.

After 20 minutes of routine driving, the magic moment arrived. The road was free of other traffic and I could no longer wait to hammer the throttle. The transition to full open on both four-barrel carbs was seamless. Along with the kick in the pants came a distinct howl from the carbs as they sucked in the air. Once again I refrained from yelling "YEEHAWWW!" I glanced at the speedometer and it read 110 and the big Hemi was still pulling. I backed off and slowed to the speed limit. Hemi acceleration is a drug that must be tried more than once, so I nailed it again. Once again the acceleration was smooth and strong. Now, I fully understand why the Hemi Road Runner is one of the most highly desired muscle cars. It drives beautifully and performs better than advertised. Thanks, Akbar!

cooling hardware. Plymouth made no excuses for this car's aggressive looks or lack of wheel covers. It was designed as a street racer and the mere thought of it gave auto insurance salesmen chest pains. It offered every bit of the Hemi's wheel-spinning acceleration at half the cost. It's interesting to note that in 1967, General Motors restricted multiple carburetion to only the Corvette, whereas Chrysler freely added carburetors to its muscle cars because nothing looks better under the hood of a muscle car than a big load of carburetors.

Motor Trend magazine selected the 1969 Road Runner as its *Car of the Year*. In multi-page ads decreeing the fact, Plymouth copywriters wrote extravagantly about the specific quarter-mile performance numbers their potential buyers were looking for. In stock form, a 1969 Hemi Road Runner equipped with a TorqueFlite and 4.10 rear axle consistently ran the quarter mile in the mid-13–second range at speeds of 105 miles per hour. The next day, the same car could be brought back to the track and given a few bolt-on performance additions. A Racer Brown cam and kit were added, along with a set of Hooker headers.

Top
Like the Super Bee, the 1971 Road Runner was completely restyled and featured a robustly rounded body with hidden windshield wipers and flush door handles. Color-keyed Elastomer front and rear bumpers were optional. The white stenciled lettering on the hood says, "Air Grabber."

Above insert
The optional bucket seats used in this 1971 Road Runner are the same as those used in the Dodge Charger, Super Bee, and Plymouth GTX. The Road Runner and GTX used the same instrument panel as the Dodge Charger.

The 1971 Road Runner's rounded body was accented with aggressively flared wheel openings. The dual decorative chrome exhaust tips that emerge from under the rear valance panel were standard with the Hemi engine (except in California). The black stripes on the rear were optional. Plymouth even color-keyed its bumper bolts with the body color bumpers.

When run with the headers open, the Hemi Road Runner's elapsed times dropped by seven-tenths of a second and speeds improved by five miles per hour.

The 1969 Super Bee received very few changes from the 1968 model. Although the Super Bee didn't win *Car of the Year*, it was the Road Runner's performance equal. The Bumblebee stripes were revised to a single broad stripe flanked by a pair of thin stripes that wrapped around the rear of the car. Hemi-equipped Super Bees were modified with a special Ramcharger hood. It featured twin scoops

that fed cool outside air to the engine. "Hemi" was spelled out in small chrome letters on the outboard side of each scoop. The Super Bee had another set of scoops that were strictly ornamentation. This nonfunctional pair of side scoops was attached to the quarter panel. There was also a 440 Six-Pack version of the Super Bee in 1969 that had the same elements as the Road Runner's package.

Compared to 1968, overall sales of the 1969 Road Runner almost doubled, and sales of the 1969 Super Bee more than tripled. Road Runner Hemi sales were as follows: 422 hardtops, 356 coupes,

and 10 convertibles. There were 258 Hemi Super Bees sold in 1969: 92 hardtops and 166 coupes.

The Road Runner and Super Bee were both given a major facelift in 1970. The only remaining exterior body components carried over from 1969 were the roof and doors. New quarter panels, taillight treatment, and an entirely new front end were added. The Road Runner's quarter panels featured gently rounded corners and had a small nonfunctional scoop on the side. A Power

Dome hood replaced the twin vertical vents. The new Air Grabber scoop was standard on the Hemi-equipped Road Runners. With the flip of a switch, the driver could open this scoop. Once open, the clever graphics of a toothy character, similar to the nose art on the Flying Tiger's P-40 fighters, could be seen.

Imagine this scene on Woodward Avenue 30 years ago: a young guy driving a Camaro pulls up alongside a new Road Runner stopped at a traffic light. The Camaro driver looks over and points down the road—the international sign for "Wanna race?" The Road Runner driver smiles, nods, and casually reaches down to open the Air Grabber scoop. The Road Runner is already ahead on style points and is about to demonstrate to the poor guy in the Camaro why he should have stayed home that night.

The Dodge Super Bee's 1970 restyle included a unique front-end treatment. Twin nostril-like grilles were divided by a wide center split. Each side of the grille was surrounded by a halo-style chrome bumper. The irregular shape of the halo bumper and the wide center split seemed out of step with the clean, symmetrical lines Dodge designers had been laying down. Super Bees were available in a two-door coupe or hardtop.

In 1970, Bumblebee stripes were again part of the Super Bee option in an expanded color selection. Or, as an alternative, the customer could opt for a different set of stripes. These stripes are known as the "reverse C-stripes" and consisted of two hockey-stick stripes that outlined the quarter panel's character lines. A larger circular Super Bee decal was placed where the stripes joined at the rear of the car. The last year in which the Super Bee would be based on the Coronet model was 1970.

In 1968 and 1969, 15-inch-diameter wheels were a standard part of the Road Runner and Super Bee Hemi package. In 1970, they were no longer required and all Hemis came standard with 14x6-inch wheels and F70x14-inch tires. The 15-inch wheels became an option and were only available with F60x15-inch white-letter tires.

In 1970, the enthusiasm for high-powered muscle cars was starting to decline. Customers wanted cars that looked fast, but didn't want to pay the high tariffs for insurance that were required with the 400-plus-horsepower engines. A portion of high-performance sales may have gone to the new Plymouth and Dodge E-body offerings: the Barracuda and Challenger. In 1970, only 159 buyers specified a Hemi engine out of the total 36,327 Road Runners sold. Sales in 1970 for the Super Bee were 14,254 units and only 36 of those were equipped with a Hemi.

The 1971 Plymouth Road Runner was based on the all-new Satellite Sebring that replaced the Belvedere. This new body was released only as a hardtop and shared the same 115-inch-wheel-base platform as the new 1971 Dodge Charger, on which the

THE COMPETITION

Of all the cars that Chrysler produced, the Road Runner and Super Bee had the toughest competition. They both were latecomers to the muscle car party. The other guests had arrived and had the run of the place. The GTO had a five-year jump on them and the SS 396 Chevelle was into its third year of production. These two cars, along with the Olds 442, Ford Fairlane GT, and Mercury Cyclone, owned the performance image market until 1968.

In 1968, the most powerful engine that could be bought in the freshly restyled GTO was the 400-ci Ram Air II, rated at 366 horsepower. The 1968 Chevelle also received a new skin and its top-rated SS 396 model boasted 375 horsepower. Ford's Torino could be ordered with the 360-horsepower, 428-ci engine, and the Hurst Olds 442 had a 455-ci engine that developed 390 horsepower.

In 1969 Chevrolet unleashed its COPO (Central Office Production Order) plan, where a high-performance 427 could be specified for a Chevelle. The aluminum-headed Corvette L-72, conservatively rated at 425 horsepower, could be specified in an SS Chevelle. Although it was the performance match of a Hemi Road Runner, obtaining one of these special-order Chevelles was not easy and a lot more expensive. In response to the Road Runner, Pontiac created the GTO Judge in 1969.

By 1970 the competition was experiencing a cubic inch frenzy. While Ford topped out at 429, Buick, Olds, and Pontiac all had their high-performance 455 engines. Chevrolet offered two versions of the Super Sport Chevelle: an SS 396 and an SS 454. Dollar for dollar, the 1970 LS-6 450-horsepower SS 454 was the closest competition to the Hemi Road Runner. Like the Hemi engine for the Road Runner, the LS-6 could be selected as an option at any Chevy dealer—no special COPO document needed. The Hemi's final year in 1971 saw a decline in horsepower ratings from all the competitors as compression ratios were cut to make way for low-lead gas. Everyone detuned except for the Hemi.

Super Bee was based. Even though they had the same wheelbase, the Dodge Super Bee was 2.2 inches longer.

Similar in size to the 1970 models, these new bodies appeared larger and were definitely more rounded. The front end featured a long, low hood line that extended back to the windshield to effectively hide the windshield wipers under its rear edge. Up front was a flush-fitting, halo-style bumper (or bumpers on the Road Runner) with headlights that were sunk into the grille.

The square, full-wheel openings on the Road Runner flared out slightly. Dodge designers went in a different direction and used rounded wheel openings. They accentuated the body's Coke-bottle shape to define the front fenders and quarter panels.

The fender forms on both cars, along with a wider track, gave these new offerings a very aggressive look.

Body-colored bumpers were offered as an option on the 1971 Road Runner and Super Bee. These bumpers were not simply sprayed with the body color, but were coated with Elastomer, similar to those offered on the new Plymouth Barracuda and Dodge Challenger. A transverse strobe stripe was optional on the 1971 Road Runner. It ran from the rear wheel opening forward across the C-pillar and roof, and then back down the C-pillar to the other rear wheel opening. With the Hemi engine, the Air Grabber hood was standard on both the Road Runner and Super Bee.

The base engine for both the 1971 Road Runner and Super Bee was a downsized 383, rated at 300 horsepower. It was a move prompted by emission laws and pressure from the insurance industry. The addition of an optional 340-ci engine also allowed the Road Runner to qualify for lower insurance premiums. The Hemi was still on the option list, but there were fewer brave souls willing to shoulder the extra cost of the engine and the subsequent exorbitant insurance premium associated with it. A total of 55 Hemi-powered Road Runners and 22 Hemi-powered Super Bees were sold in 1971.

In the early 1970s, Chrysler had a good friend in *Motor Trend* magazine. Having purchased zero advertising space in the December 1970 issue, Chrysler still garnered the cover and close to 10 pages of internal positive editorial copy. On the cover was a bright red 1971 Super Bee charging directly at the camera with two other 1971 Dodge Chargers following in close pursuit, all stirring up clouds of high-speed dust. The featured article in that issue covered the new Dodges. There was also a two-page 1971 Barracuda buyer's guide.

Two Charger models, a 500 and an SE and two Super Bees, were compared in an article titled "The Chargers Of The Dodge Brigade." There was a wide variety of engines tested among the four cars. The Charger 500 was powered by a 383 and the Charger SE had a 370-horsepower 440 under the hood. While well equipped, the two Chargers were pedestrian models optioned more for comfort than for speed. On the other hand, the Super Bees were built for action. One was equipped with a 385-horsepower 440, and the other a Hemi.

As tested, the two 1971 Dodge Super Bees each listed at a base price of $3,245. Each was optioned with the Super Track Pak at an additional $219.30. This option was only available with the 440 or Hemi engine and included 4.10 gears for the Dana rear axle and front disc brakes. This was an addition to the Track Pak option (heavy-duty radiator, seven-bladed torque-drive fan, and dual-point distributor) that came standard with both high-performance engines. Both cars were equipped with power steering, TorqueFlite transmission, hood pins, and a tachometer.

From there, the options varied with each car, but nothing too far from what the mainstream automotive enthusiast of 1971 would order on a performance car. The big difference was the cost of the 385-horsepower 440 Six-Pack at $262.15 versus the Hemi's almost painful $883.55 addition to the list price. Looking back today with the value of Hemi cars, the price difference seems almost insignificant, but in 1971, $883 could buy a lot of groceries or pay a few months' worth of rent. The total list price for the Hemi Super Bee was $4,966.20, and the 440 Super Bee was $4,702.30.

Motor Trend writer A. B. Shuman gave the Charger-based cars high marks in various categories, only dinging them for their overall large size. When it came to his comments about the Hemi Super Bee, Shuman said it was "remarkable." His biggest beef was with the carburetor linkage. He felt the stiff detent at 1/4 throttle, where the second carburetor is called into action, which made the throttle difficult to control on the drag strip. On the positive side, Shuman said the detent on the throttle linkage allowed him to stay out of the secondaries, while cruising normally. With this restriction, he was still able to cruise at 70 miles per hour with the 4.10 gears, while turning 4,000 rpm. He boasted about the Hemi's "miserly" fuel economy of 11.4 miles per gallon, but at the time, gas was plentiful and even the smallest compacts could barely register 20 miles per gallon.

The *Motor Trend* Hemi Super Bee shined on the track. Its slowest run down the quarter was 14.18 seconds. This was accomplished with the TorqueFlite's gear selector in Drive. Shifted manually at 5,800 rpm—and with the top of the air cleaner removed—the car's elapsed time (e.t.) dropped to 13.73 seconds at a speed of 104.0 miles per hour. In comparison, the 440 Super Bee ran the quarter in 14.74 seconds at a speed of 97.3 miles per hour. In his summation, Shuman wrote, "The funny thing about the Hemi Super Bee was that, even before testing, we had the feeling that it was going to be strong. The result was that there was never any need to cob it to impress the other guy. It was a Hemi and you knew it ... that was enough."

The Hemi Super Bee tested in that *Motor Trend* article is alive and well and featured in this book. It was originally purchased by a man who read the *Motor Trend* article, went to his local Dodge dealership, and demanded to have "that car." He had to pay for the car in advance, but he finally got it. It was one of the many Hemi cars that were too good to get rid of, so it was placed in storage. Like many Hemi cars, it survived and changed hands a few times. In January 2002, it was sold unrestored at auction for $80,000.

In 1971, the curtain came down on the Super Bee. Even though the Road Runner would be produced through 1975, the Super Bee was more beauty than beast. With the Hemi gone and stricter emission laws in effect, the Road Runner's performance

BEEP BEEP

Between 1969 and 1971, all Road Runner horns were painted light purple and had a "Voice of the Road Runner" decal applied. This horn added the distinctive Beep Beep sound to the car.

When Plymouth created the 1968 Road Runner, they also added the little cartoon bird's distinctive "beep-beep" voice to the car. A special horn built by Sparton (one of Chrysler's suppliers of regular horns) mimicked the bird's characteristic beep-beep voice. Most domestic cars built in the 1960s were fitted with dual horns, one of which emitted a high tone and the other a low tone. The result was a harmonious resonance. The Road Runner had only one horn with this unique sound.

The horn on the 1968 Road Runner was painted black. Near the end of the 1968 production run, a decal was added to the horn that read, "Voice of the Road Runner." In 1969, the Road Runner's horn was painted a light purple and retained the decal. This horn was used through 1974, the end of the Road Runner production year.

While the horn on a vehicle is only one small component, it represented a big piece of the Road Runner's character. It was the perfect tie-in to the cartoon bird, and because there was only one horn instead of two, it cost less to produce. Like the cartoon character on which the car was based, the horn proved to the buying public that Plymouth didn't take itself too seriously.

was limited. Between 1976 and 1980 Plymouth offered a Road Runner option group on its Volare—a sad ending to a proud name.

The Plymouth Road Runner and Dodge Super Bee were two of the most highly identifiable vehicles of the muscle car era. They were designed strictly for performance and marketed to those who found going through the gears in a street race the ultimate thrill. Their aggressive good looks made cruising through the local burger stand almost as much fun as racing. In addition to being affordable, the Hemi engine was an option. What more could a motorhead ask for?

CHAPTER FIVE

HEMI CHARGERS

1966–1971

In the mid- and late 1950s, Chrysler had always been in step with or a step ahead of automotive design trends. Its pink and black or tri-toned painted cars, along with its sharp-edged fins, set the styling trends of the decade. By the early 1960s, Chrysler had lost its edge. Sales for 1962 were down, largely due to the public's poor response to the gawky look of the Plymouths and Dodges. In 1961, Virgil Exner, the dean of Chrysler's beautiful designs of the 1950s, was replaced by Elwood Engle. Engle had been a Ford designer and was the father of the stunning 1961 Lincoln Continental. It was his job to reshape the look of Chrysler products for the next decade. Engle cut off the fins and removed all of Exner's styling cues by the 1963 model year. Exner, now head of his own design firm, said that Engle's designs looked like "plucked chickens," but sales were good in 1963 and the public was pleased with the cleaner lines of the Dodge and Plymouth. Engle's design philosophy included giving the cars a "heavier" look.

Engle was acutely aware of Ford's intention to build the Mustang, and over at GM, work was beginning on the Olds Toronado. With these cars in the works, Engle was required to develop two completely new cars for Chrysler—a sporty Plymouth Barracuda to compete against the Mustang, and an upscale Dodge Charger. The Charger name first appeared on a 1964 Dodge show car that was constructed from a customized Polara. It was converted into a two-passenger convertible model with a small wraparound windscreen and large

When the Dodge Charger was redesigned in 1968, it became an instant classic because of its beautiful lines. Its beauty was also its nemesis, and minor changes had to be made to the exterior to make it competitive in NASCAR racing. This 1969 Dodge Charger 500 is one of the 500 vehicles modified that year and sold to the general public in order to comply with NASCAR rules. The Charger 500s were equipped with a 440 or Hemi engine.

Dodge stylists did a masterful job of using the Coronet's basic sheet metal to create the 1966 Charger. The lines were crisp and clean. This 1966 model was originally equipped with full wheel covers and Blue Streak tires. Chrome Road Wheels and red-line tires were available in 1966.

The Dodge Charger was introduced in 1966 and was designed to compete in the emerging personal luxury car class. Much of the Charger's styling, including its dramatic sloped roof, came from Dodge's Charger II show car. The quarter panels were similar to those of the 1966 Coronet, except for the larger wheel opening. There were 468 Chargers built with the Hemi engine for 1966.

The instrument panel for the 1966 Charger featured four circular chrome pods. The 6,000-rpm tachometer is on the right of the 150-mile-per-hour speedometer.

aerodynamic headrests. In 1965, the Charger II show car was introduced. It had the imposing fastback roofline and sculpted sides that were elements of the upcoming production Charger.

Creating the production versions of the Charger and Barracuda proved to be a daunting task. Because of cost considerations, both were "make from" designs; the Barracuda was to be developed from the Valiant platform, and the Charger from the Coronet platform. To make a design statement, both the Barracuda and Charger would have a fastback roofline. Fastbacks were fashionable in the late 1930s and 1940s. Postwar sketches

for advanced 1950s models showed sleek, fastback designs, but the advent of the pillarless hardtop in the early 1950s killed the momentum of the fastback design. It took the new breed of 1960s automotive designers—Bill Mitchell at GM, and Engle at Chrysler—to revive and refine the look. Ford also helped revive

This is Dodge Charger

Watch out for the fastback that's full-sized and fully loaded. Dodge Charger is one dream car that sprang to life with all the excitement and fresh ideas intact. With styling that swivels heads in your neighborhood as fast and often as it did in auto shows a year ago. With comfort that won't quit and standard features that usually cost extra—tach, a racing-style steering wheel, bucket seats all around. Plus power choices all the way up to the hot, optional 426 Street Hemi. Leave it to Dodge to do things right, right? So do right by yourself. Check out Charger, the Dodge Rebellion's hot new leader that's stirring up excitement on streets and highways everywhere. Do it now. The Dodge Rebellion wants you.

Dodge Charger

DODGE DIVISION ✦ CHRYSLER MOTORS CORPORATION

Put down undersized, underequipped personal cars ...go Charger.

The 1966 Charger was the centerpiece of Chrysler's "Dodge Rebellion" advertising campaign. This print ad used a dramatic rear view that accentuated the Charger's fastback roof.

the movement with its fastback 1963 Galaxie 500XL and Mercury Marauder that were both designed for NASCAR racing. A "make from" car with a fastback roofline is the easiest to build, but the general public thinks that the car is all new. All it takes is a new roof, deck lid, and a few mix-and-match trim pieces.

The new Dodge Charger would be built on the company's 117-inch wheelbase, B-body platform. When work started on the Charger, a good portion of the new Coronet's development had been completed. The Dodge design team was asked to create a distinctive car with a fastback roofline that would

sticker for around $3,500, and was to be built from the Coronet. Required components to be taken from the Coronet included the cowl, windshield, and hardtop doors. The principal exterior stylist responsible for the Charger's design was Carl "Cam" Cameron.

The car Cameron was designing would lead Dodge's 1966 "Rebellion" advertising theme. It would be the cornerstone of Dodge's new image of style and performance. The Charger would compete against the Olds Toronado, Buick Riviera, and Ford Thunderbird. Because the Charger was built on the Coronet platform and could share many of its components, it was less costly to build than its luxury competitors. It would also have all of the Coronet's high-performance options, including the new 1966, street Hemi engine in 1966.

Because of the Charger's hardtop design, a considerable amount of body structure had to be added in the area of the C-pillars and upper rear deck area in order to keep the body rigid. Small but significant changes were made to the Coronet's quarter panels for the Charger. The rear wheel openings were raised and shaped the same as the front wheel openings. The large, mildly flared wheel openings gave the Charger an aggressive, sporty look. Two horizontal depressions, which simulated air intakes, were added to the leading edge of the quarter panel. The sculpted sides of the Charger were devoid of any trim, other than a narrow beltline molding, a rocker panel molding, and thin wheel lip moldings. On the large triangular sail panel was a Charger nameplate.

Up front, the Charger's rectangular full-width grille was a series of thin vertical bars. Hidden behind the vertical bars at each end of the large grille opening were the parking/turn signals. Inboard of those lights were the hidden quad headlights. Carefully disguised within the grille's thin bars were the headlight doors. From a short distance it was impossible to distinguish the headlight doors hidden within the grille's network of bars. When the headlights were open, the bezels surrounding the lights were fully trimmed with vertical bars that blended with the grille. No other manufacturer had so elegantly executed a hidden-headlight design.

Twin electric motors, geared down to 450:1, rotated the lights. When the light switch was pulled to the full ON position, the lights would rotate into position. During the transition, a red light was illuminated on the instrument panel until the lights were in place. There was also an override switch that allowed the lights to be rotated into position at any time. This was used when the headlights were being washed, or in icy climates, to prevent the headlight doors from freezing shut. A simple chrome-plated beam front bumper complemented the clean front-end design.

The only exterior difference between the 1966 and 1967 Charger was the addition of small, front fender turn-signal indicators. There were several mechanical changes made to comply with new automobile safety laws, including a collapsible steering column. A new 440 Magnum V-8 was added to the option list, which resulted in diminished Hemi sales for 1967. This 1967 Dodge Charger is one of 118 equipped with the street Hemi engine.

The rear of the Charger mimicked the front with a wide rectangular one-piece taillight with "Charger" spelled out in chrome letters across the width of the red lens. The rear bumper was similar to the front, except that the ends slightly swept up to the quarter panel. To keep the integrity of the full-width taillight, backup lights were placed in the rear bumper on each side of the license plate. Bright exterior trim was limited to a thin beltline molding, slender wheel moldings, and a rocker panel molding. The 1966 Charger design elements made it look long, low, and wide. The Chrysler design staff's execution of the Charger's exterior sheet metal was clean and fashionable.

The new Charger's interior was as contemporary and sporty as its sleek exterior. It featured individual seating for four covered

The only way to get a Hemi in a 1969 Dodge Charger was to specify the R/T model. All R/Ts came standard with rear Bumblebee stripes that could be deleted. Although the Rallye Wheels on this 1969 Charger look good, they were actually not available until 1970.

Above

Hidden headlights were retained on the second-generation Dodge Charger. The grille and headlight doors were made of plastic and were recessed deeply into the front of the car. R/T Chargers received a small "R/T" emblem on the left headlight door.

Below

The interior of the 1969 Charger looked as efficient as a race car. Two large circular gauges for the 150-mile-per-hour speedometer and combination clock/tachometer were in front of the driver. To the right were four smaller circular gauges for fuel, alternator, temperature, and oil pressure. All of the switches were rocker-type. The Hurst shifter was standard with the four-speed transmission, but the console was optional.

Above

If Bumblebee stripes were deleted from a 1969 Charger R/T, a small chrome "R/T" emblem was added to the quarter panel. The flip-top gas filler was on the top of the left quarter panel. Dodge designers wanted one gas cap on each side but had to settle for one on the left side.

Right

In 1969, Dodge changed the grille of the Charger and added a small center split. When a Hemi was ordered, it came standard with 15-inch wheels, dog-dish hubcaps, and F70-15 red-line tires. The F6HEMI license plate refers to this car's Bright Green paint code and the engine under the hood.

The 1969 Charger 500 was built to counter the aerodynamic advantages that the Ford Torino Talladega enjoyed. One of the changes made to these special Chargers was the removal of the tunnel back rear window. This helped reduce turbulence over the rear deck. The Bumblebee stripes were similar to the ones on the R/T, except for the "500" cutouts.

In order to smooth the airflow over the windshield, special A-pillar covers were installed on the Charger 500s. All Hemi-equipped 1969 Dodge Chargers, including 52 Charger 500s, received a small "Hemi" emblem on the door.

in padded Cologne-grain vinyl in blue, saddle tan, red, white, black, or citron gold. Up front were Chrysler's new clamshell-design bucket seats. These seats were gracefully curved and trimmed with thin chrome moldings. The rear seats were also buckets with backrests that could fold flat.

Luggage capacity was increased to over 7 feet in length with both rear seats and the center armrest folded down. A diecast, chrome-plated console divided the seating area. A floor-mounted shifter was standard on all 1966 Chargers with either the four-speed manual or TorqueFlite automatic transmission. Only the base 318 engine with the standard three-speed manual was column shifted. On the console in front of the shifter was a clock that was

Chryslers B-bodies, including the Dodge Charger, were redesigned in 1971. The Charger's Coke-bottle shape was retained and improved upon with the addition of ventless door glass, hidden windshield wipers, and flush door handles. The R/T continued to be the performance model with a standard 440 engine and optional 440 Six-Pack or Hemi engines.

mounted in a chrome-plated housing. The Charger's instrument panel was a basic Coronet unit with four additional circular gauge pods positioned in front of the driver. Full instrumentation within those pods included a 6,000-rpm tachometer. The instrument panel was illuminated with electroluminescent lighting, a bulbless illumination system that was developed for the 1960–1962 Chryslers. In keeping with the Charger's sporty theme, the steering wheel was a three-spoke design with a simulated woodgrain rim. The headliner was a one-piece fiberglass component that did little to absorb noise.

Dodge established the Charger's performance image with its selection of standard and optional V-8 engines. The base engine was the 318-ci, 230-horsepower V-8. Three optional engines were available: the 361-ci 265-horsepower V-8, the 383-ci 325-horse-power V-8, and the new-for-1966 street Hemi. Along with the Hemi engine came a heavy-duty suspension, which featured 11-inch brake drums. Like all other 1966 Hemi cars, the Charger rolled on 7.75x14-inch blue-streak tires. These were mounted on 5.5-inch-wide steel wheels fitted with a special full-wheel cover.

The new Dodge Charger was first seen by millions of viewers in a television commercial on January 1, 1966, during the Rose Bowl game. Charger sales were good, but not great, for a car introduced well into the model year. A total of 37,344 were produced, and 468 were Hemi-equipped.

When ordered with a Hemi, a "426 Hemi" emblem was placed on the side of the front fender. Those who ordered the Hemi gave up the 5/50 warranty for a 12-month, 12,000-mile version that was limited to the original owner. While everyone liked the exterior, the Charger was criticized for its basic Coronet underpinnings. Its smooth exterior and Hemi engine succeeded in helping

The Ramcharger hood was standard with the Hemi in the 1971 Dodge Charger R/T. The driver could open this trapdoor-style scoop at any time. Drivers opened this hood most frequently when racing or when cruising through a drive-in restaurant.

Below
All 1971 Dodge Charger R/Ts, including those painted black, received a special black hood decal that covered the Power Bulge hood. Hidden headlights were no longer standard and optional only on certain Charger models. Hood pins were also optional.

NASCAR racers: David Pearson won the 1966 season title in a Dodge Charger.

Only minor changes were made to the exterior of the 1967 Charger. The biggest change was under the hood, where the 375-horsepower, 400-ci engine was an available option. This gave the buyer the opportunity to have Hemi like performance at half the cost.

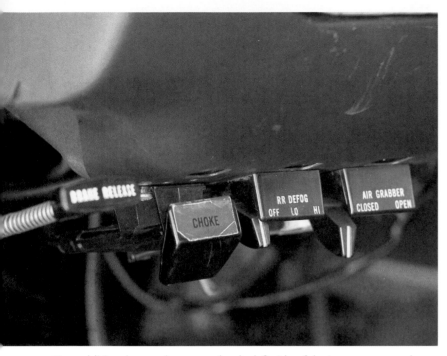

Two additional controls were under the left side of the instrument panel on Hemi-equipped 1971 Dodge Chargers. The red handle on the left was the manual choke control for the carburetor. The switch that opened the hood scoop was on the right.

Responding to critics, who felt a car of the Charger's size should seat more than four, designers added an optional center "mother-in-law" seat. This consisted of a fixed center cushion that could be converted to a center armrest by folding down the seat's backrest. The two individual buckets with fold-down seat backs were retained in the rear. When a console, now optional, was specified, it ended at the back of the front seats to give the rear-seat passengers a full-width floor.

New for 1967 were the optional 14x5.5-inch-wide chrome-plated road wheels and five-spoke simulated mag wheel hubcaps. Red-line tires were also new for 1967 and were standard with the Hemi or 440.

Dodge expected the Charger to sell well in its second year, but it didn't. Total sales for 1967 were half those of the previous year and only 118 Hemi Chargers were sold. At a list price of $3,128, it was well positioned to grab sales away from the Buick Riviera, priced at $4,469, or from the Olds Toronado, priced at $4,674. The Charger was only $300 more than the Cougar XR7. It was a problem that would be resolved in 1968 with a revolutionary design.

For 1968, Chrysler designers were determined to make the Charger look completely different from the Coronet. They wanted a car that would look at home parked in front of a fine restaurant in New York, driving on a Los Angeles freeway, or racing on the high-banks of Daytona. The new Charger had to be stylish, sporty, and aggressive.

Several members of the design staff submitted sketches of the new Charger to Bill Brownlie. The ones he liked best were those created by Richard Tighstin. Tighstin's vision was of a car with a narrow front end that became wider toward the rear. From the side, the car had a definite wedge shape and a spoiler on the rear.

The second-generation Charger had a distinctive Coke-bottle shape. It carried the same full-width rectangular grille and full-wheel openings as its predecessor. Unlike the original Charger, this one was smoothly shaped with rounded sides and a new, tunneled rear window. The new Charger had the right combination of sex appeal and muscle.

From nose to tail, the Charger was completely new and featured no Coronet body components. The wheel openings were full and the sheet metal around the wheel openings was pulled up and out, to give the car its Coke-bottle shape.

Two simulated reverse vents were stamped into the outer skin on the front edge of each door. These reverse vents were also used on the hood. These vents were originally designed to be functional, but the idea was nixed over concerns about water draining into the engine compartment and heat from the engine being drawn into the interior through the cowl vent. Instead, optional turn-signal indicators were located in each of the hood depressions.

The 1968 Charger's front-end treatment was masterful. It retained the rectangular opening of the previous Charger, but narrowed the opening to make the car appear wider. The thin vertical grille bars were deeply recessed. Hidden headlights were retained, but cost-saving measures dictated that the headlight doors should be made of plastic and that they simply flip up by means of a vacuum actuator to reveal the fixed quad headlights. Accenting the front end was a thin, blade-style bumper. Beneath it was a body-color valance panel that also housed the parking lights.

The roof and rear-end treatment deviated from the 1966–1967 Charger's design theme. In place of the severe fastback, the 1968 Charger's roofline included long sail panels with a recessed back window. This type of roof was first seen on the 1966 GM intermediate hardtops. It allows a swoopy roofline and retains a conventional-sized luggage compartment.

In the rear, the full-width taillight of the 1966 and 1967 models gave way to two pairs of round lights set into an angled panel. A thin, bright molding surrounds this panel. Across the rear of the car was a built-in spoiler. The rear bumper was as thin as the front and it also had a body-color lower valance panel. One of the little details that gave the 1968 Charger its distinction was the flip-top gas cap located on top of the left quarter panel.

The car was originally designed to have one on each side, but that feature was eliminated when the Charger reached the production stage of development.

The interior of the 1968 Charger was not as ground breaking as the original Charger's had been. All-vinyl bucket seats were standard in front, with a bench seat in the rear that was available in blue, green, red, black, gold, or white. A fixed center cushion with a folding armrest was optional to give the Charger seating for six passengers. The console was also optional, and when selected, that was where the four-speed or TorqueFlite shifter was located. Dodge touted the Charger's instrument panel as "sports-car-type." Directly in front of the driver were two large dials, which housed the 150-miles-per-hour speedometer and clock. When an optional tachometer was specified, it was integrated into the clock. To the right were four smaller circular gauges for fuel, oil pressure, water temperature, and ammeter. The switches were rocker style, or thumb wheels.

The chassis and engine combinations for the 1968 Charger were carryovers from 1967. A new model was added to the Charger in 1968—the R/T (Road and Track). Billed strictly as a performance package, it offered a standard 375-horsepower, 440-ci engine, and a host of heavy-duty components.

TorqueFlite was the standard transmission on the R/T, with a four-speed manual as an option. Rear Bumblebee stripes were standard, but could be deleted. The Hemi engine was only available with the Charger R/T package and in 1968, 475 were sold. When a Hemi engine was selected, a small "Hemi" emblem was added to the door. In 1968, all Chrysler Hemi-equipped cars were fitted with 15x6-inch steel wheels. The stylish Charger followed form and these wheels were fitted with F70x15-inch red-stripe tires and dog-dish hubcaps.

The Dodge Charger stepped into a different automotive class in 1968. Instead of competing against luxury cars, it developed into more of a sports sedan, and competed against the Pontiac Grand Prix. Its redesign was a bold step forward for Chrysler and was only overshadowed in the automotive market in 1968 by the redesigned Corvette.

Very few changes distinguished the 1969 Charger from the 1968 model. Most notable was the addition of a center split in the grille, a new pair of rectangular-shaped taillights, and revised side marker lights. The Hemi engine was again only available with the R/T option, and in 1969, 432 were delivered.

While the new Charger looked as if it would be as fast as Superman, its on-track aerodynamic performance was more like that of Clark Kent. Hindering the Charger's performance was its deep-set grille and tunneled rear window. The deep-set front grille acted as an air scoop. Once inside the grille cavity at high speed, air had nowhere to go and created lift. A small front spoiler reduced some of the lift, but it was only an ineffective solution to a much bigger problem. The tunnel back roof also caused lift at high speeds.

To address these aerodynamic problems, Chrysler modified a 1968 Charger, and named it the Charger 500. It was first introduced in June 1968, at Chrysler's Proving Grounds and was released as a 1969 model. Creative Industries, a Detroit-area fabrication shop, modified 500 cars for sale to the public, the number required by NASCAR to make the modifications legal on the track. The intent of NASCAR's rule was to prevent auto manufacturers from building cars for racing that were not otherwise available to the general public. The Charger 500 featured a Coronet grille, with exposed headlights, that was mounted flush with the front edge of the hood and fenders. Smooth stainless covers hid the A-pillars. A plug was made for the rear window that followed the sloping shape of the C-pillars. This flush-mounted rear window required a special shortened deck lid. On the rear was a Bumblebee stripe with the number "500" on the side of the quarter panel. Red-stripe F70x15-inch tires were standard and white-streak tires were a no-cost option.

The Charger 500s were equipped with a 375-horsepower, 440-ci engine or the optional Hemi. TorqueFlite or Hurst-shifted four-speed manual transmissions were the only two transmissions available. Only 67 Charger 500s were built with Hemi power. *Hot Rod* magazine had scheduled three Hemi-powered Charger 500s for a road test for their February 1969 issue. Just prior to the evaluation, one of the Chargers was stolen, which left one four-speed and one TorqueFlite to test. The author, Steve Kelly, favored the Hemi 500 equipped with TorqueFlite, and wrote, "This is the kind of car you make excuses to drive." He heartily recommended the optional front disc brakes. At the drag strip, the four-speed car ran the best times at 13.48 seconds and a speed of 109 miles per hour. The TorqueFlite-equipped Hemi Charger 500 ran the quarter in 13.8 seconds at a speed of 105 miles per hour.

Any performance advancements the Dodge Charger 500 had made in aerodynamics had also been made by Ford and Mercury. The Charger 500 was about to face the Torino Talladega and the Mercury Cyclone Spoiler at the biggest race of the year—the Daytona 500.

The 1969 Daytona 500 was another turning point for the Chrysler racing effort. The Charger 500 was out-gunned by LeeRoy Yarbrough's Torino Talladega. To remain competitive, Chrysler pulled out all the stops with the winged Charger Daytona. Originally planned as a 1970 model, it was pulled ahead to 1969 (see chapter 6 for the full story).

The most notable changes to the 1970 Dodge Charger were the redesigned grille and front bumper. The doors on the R/T received a large vertical reversed scoop, which was located at the

The rear of the 1971 Charger followed the same theme as the front of the car, with a halo-style bumper. At a price of $3,223, the 1971 Charger R/T was a performance bargain. The vinyl roof and rear spoiler were options available at additional cost.

forward edge covering the stamped depressions. As in the previous two years, the Hemi engine was only available in the R/T, and only 112 were sold.

A new addition to the engine lineup was the 440 Six-Pack engine rated at 375 horsepower. With the exception of a cast-iron manifold to replace the aluminum manifold, it was the same engine that had been installed in the Road Runner and Super Bee.

In 1971, Dodge completely restyled the Charger. It shared the same platform as the Coronet, but still had the aggressive good looks to appeal to the muscle car buyer. Even though its wheelbase was 2 inches shorter than the 1970 model, the new Charger looked longer. The new Charger had a forward raked profile that was attributed to a raised beltline. The ventless side glass seemed to clean up the side's lines.

The Charger retained the Coke-bottle–shaped body and full wheel openings, but the roof no longer had the tunneled rear window. The new Charger's grille was rectangular in shape, and surrounded by a halo bumper with a large center split. Hidden headlights were now optional on all the models except the base Charger.

The R/T and Super Bee were the performance models of the 1971 Charger. The R/T featured a domed and louvered hood with flat black accents. When the optional Hemi was ordered, the louvers were deleted in favor of a Ramcharger hood, which was

optional with the 440 engine. This is the first appearance of any type of cold-air package on the Charger.

Unique door outer skins that had two vertical depressions at the door's leading edge were used on the R/T. Inside the depressions were black tape accents. The R/T also featured a black side body stripe that ran from the rear edge of the hood along the beltline and terminated at the end of the quarter panel. The door and side stripes could be deleted.

Small R/T emblems were added to the sides of the front fenders and to the rear edge of the deck lid. The Charger R/T also had special taillight lenses that were divided into three segments per side. Only 63 Dodge 1971 Charger R/Ts were sold with the Hemi engine.

Dodge introduced several unique options on the 1971 Charger. Option A54 was a colored bumper group that included special front and rear bumpers in body color. The colors were limited to Bright Blue Metallic, Citron Yellow, Hemi Orange, Green Go, and Plum Crazy. Also available was an optional rear window louver panel. It was painted flat black and hinged at the top so it could be swung out of the way to clean the rear window. In 1971, Dodge said good-bye to the eight-track tape player and installed a stereo cassette system. An optional microphone—so drivers could record their thoughts as they drove along the road—was also available.

The Dodge Chargers have left behind an amazing legacy of style and speed. In 1966, Dodge boldly stepped into a new class of car and raised the bar for innovation by reintroducing fastback styling to full-sized cars. The 1968 Charger also set a new standard in automotive styling. Even today, a restored 1968 Charger is one of the most beautiful cars on the road.

HEMI DAYTONAS AND SUPERBIRDS

1969–1970

In the mid- to late 1960s, Ford and Chrysler were spending money on auto racing as though there were no tomorrow. Both manufacturers maximized the development of their big-cubic-inch engines and even pushed the edge of the engine design envelope with hybrid overhead cam versions. The only avenue not fully explored was that of aerodynamics. Chrysler made an initial stab at it with the Charger 500 to counter Ford's Talladega, but Chrysler's engineers knew they needed to do more to take full advantage of the powerful Hemi engine on the high-banked NASCAR tracks.

In order to improve the aerodynamic qualities of the race car, designers had to figure out how to turn the slick Dodge Charger into an airplane. The answer was to add a wing and a severely pointed nose. This directed the airflow, and the resultant downforce turned the 1969 Charger Daytona into the most outrageous and infamous of all the Chargers. The Charger Daytona was Chrysler's balls-to-the-wall approach to building an unbeatable car for NASCAR competition. The extra cost per car was $1,500, with a total cost of over $1 million dollars for the entire project.

The Dodge Charger Daytona evolved from the Charger 500 package. In an effort to correct some of the inherent aerodynamic

The 1969 Dodge Charger Daytona set the racing and muscle car worlds on their respective ears. The Daytona was Chrysler's audacious approach to improving aerodynamics in the ongoing quest to win races. To be allowed to compete with such an unusual body configuration, Dodge was required to build 500 for sale to the public. ©Randy Leffingwell

The Daytona's vertical stabilizers were not simply bolted to the top of the quarter panel, but were tied to the rear body structure with supports that ran through the trunk. The rear stripe, which also determined the wing assembly's color, was only available in white, black, or red. ©Randy Leffingwell

Above
The height of the Daytona's rear wing was determined by the clearance needed to open the deck lid. This accidental placement worked to the racer's advantage because the wing's twin uprights worked as vertical stabilizers when the cars took corners at high speed. ©Randy Leffingwell

Right
The Daytona's hidden headlights were housed within the 18-inch extended nose. A small opening on the leading edge and two small openings on the underside were the only paths directing air to the radiator. ©Randy Leffingwell

problems with the basic Charger body, Dodge made a few modifications similar to those Ford made to the Torino Talladega. The grille was pulled to the front edge of the grille opening and the rear window tunnel was replaced with a flush rear window on a panel that filled in the area between the sail panels. Smoother A-pillar moldings were also added. These changes increased on-track speeds by five miles per hour, but it still wasn't enough.

Late in 1968, meetings were held between Chrysler's aerodynamicists and the Special Vehicles Group to discuss what could be done to increase performance. It was determined that it would be necessary to smooth the front end and reduce the lift on the front end of the car. A 15 percent reduction in drag would produce 85 additional horsepower—a goal worth pursuing. Two Chrysler aerodynamicists, John Pointer and Bob Marcell, each worked on conceptual sketches. Both drawings incorporated a severely sloped nose and a high rear wing. They used the Charger 500 as the starting point for their new design.

The radical design concept was submitted for approval. When it reached Bob McCurry, Dodge's vice president and general

manager, he commented on the homely looks of the car. Then McCurry asked the crucial question: "Will it win races?" Once assured that it would be successful on the track, he gave the project a green light.

To conform to NASCAR racing guidelines, Dodge had to produce 500 Dodge Daytonas for sale to the general public by September 1, 1969, with an introduction date of April. While aerodynamic work continued, Creative Industries, a Detroit-area specialty shop, was selected to build the components for racing and was asked to modify the Daytonas to be sold to the public.

Two wind tunnels were used in the development; 3/8 scale models were run in the Wichita State wind tunnel, and full-sized mockups were run in the Lockheed-Georgia facility. The first

attempt at a new nose design was a 9-inch extension to the front, but it was then lengthened to 18 inches. The 18-inch design afforded better directional stability and lower drag. It also provided a large enough plane for the placement of headlights on the street models.

To properly balance the car, a rear aerodynamic device was needed. A deck-mounted spoiler of the appropriate size would have been as large as a barn door and effectively killed the benefits of the front-end work. A wing was determined to be a better solution. The first wing was placed 12 inches off the rear deck. One of the design considerations was the necessity (on street models) to open the deck lid wide enough to remove the spare tire. To remove the spare, the wing had to be at least 23.5 inches off the deck. With that increased height, it was determined that the wing's supports should have streamlined fairings.

The vertical fairings helped create directional stability, and the wing could exert as much as 600 pounds of downforce. Small reverse scoops were added over the front tires for tire clearance, but they stirred an immense amount of controversy over their possible aerodynamic advantage.

Within any major automaker, styling is king. Designs created within a company's design center are sacred and it takes an act of congress to get a small portion of any design changed. Although, with the Daytona program, Chrysler's stylists were the last ones to be consulted. Upon seeing the mockup, the stylists immediately wanted to make changes. McCurry came to the car's defense and

Above
The Superbird's aerodynamic additions dropped the Road Runner's coefficient of drag to 0.32. This number wasn't as good as the Charger Daytona's 0.29, because the Dodge Charger was originally designed to be more aerodynamically clean.

Left
The Road Runner's small, quarter-panel scoop fits well in the overall racy look of the Superbird. The "Plymouth" graphics on the quarter panel are the same as those used on the Superbird race cars. They were only available in black, red, or white, depending on the exterior color of the car.

Left

Reversed scoops on top of the front fenders were for tire clearance on the race cars, but they were purely cosmetic on the Superbird. The front of the Road Runner hood, which was actually a Dodge Coronet hood, had to be extended to meet the nosepiece. Hood pins were standard, and a smooth A-pillar trim was added.

Below

Two long lines of Superbirds await shipment to Plymouth dealerships. Sales of Superbirds lagged and some sat on showroom floors for a year before they were sold. Today, they're coveted by Mopar collectors everywhere. *DaimlerChrysler Historical Collection*

ordered styling to back off. Because styling was ignored, there were rumblings that the car would hurt Dodge's image and that it would never sell, but McCurry stuck to his guns. With the Dodge Daytona, function (racing) would take precedence over form (styling).

The Dodge Daytona was introduced to the press on April 13, 1969. It featured a hastily modified Charger 500 with a fiberglass nose and spoiler. The headlight doors were traced on the nose's surface with black tape. Posts supported the rear wing instead of streamlined fairings, and curiosity focused on the small reversed scoops on the front fenders. Members of the press loved the Daytona and soon there were orders for more than 1,000 cars.

Only 503 Charger Daytonas were built due to lack of time and cost. Creative Industries had to have all of the production versions completed and shipped to the dealers by September 1, 1969. Production at Creative Industries started with 2 or 3 cars per day, and eventually increased to 20 cars per day. Within three months, they had assembled all of the production cars. During this same time, Creative Industries was also making the Daytona parts kit used by the racers to convert a Charger 500 into a Daytona.

The Charger Daytona was the muscle car bargain of the decade. It listed for $3,993. Only two engines were available in the Daytona: a 375-horsepower 440, or the Hemi (of which 70 were equipped). With the exception of air conditioning, all of the other options on the lengthy list for the Charger were available. Air conditioning was not available because of the lack of airflow to the radiator, caused by the extended nose. All Charger Daytonas were marked with a wide stripe across the rear of the car and was offered in black, red, or white. This stripe was the same width as the wing and included the name "Daytona" spelled out in body color. The wing was also painted the same color as the stripe.

On the track, the Charger Daytona proved to be an excellent performer. When it made its debut at Talladega in September 1969, it quickly became the fastest stock car in history. Taking the pole at the Talladega 500 was Charlie Glotzbach with a speed of 199.466 miles-per-hour. The anticipated showdown against the Ford never materialized because the Ford drivers withdrew and cited unsafe conditions. Richard Brickhouse won the race in a Charger Daytona.

The only external Superbird components that were interchangeable with the Dodge Daytona were the headlight doors. All Superbirds had the headlight area painted flat black and the driver's-side headlight door was trimmed with a "Road Runner" decal.

1970 ROAD RUNNER SUPERBIRD

In 1968, "King" Richard Petty was anxious to hear what Plymouth was going to do involving aerodynamics for the 1969 season. Dodge would offer the slick Charger 500 and subsequent Charger Daytona and Ford would be racing its clean Talladega. The King was told that he would be racing the same Plymouth he had been racing. Petty felt he would be at a disadvantage against the aerodynamically advanced competition and asked to have a new Dodge in place of his Plymouth. His request was denied, so he switched to an anxious Ford team.

Petty's Ford won nine times in 1969 and severely damaged Plymouth's reputation. During the midseason, Petty was approached by Plymouth. They told him that if he came back in 1970, there would be a winged car for him to drive. Petty agreed to return to Plymouth in 1970 and work began on the Superbird.

Superbirds were equipped with one of two 440 Magnum engines or a street Hemi. There were 135 Superbirds equipped with a Hemi engine. There were no external badges for any of the engines. Lemon Twist was one of eight colors available for the Superbirds.

Plymouth had to construct 1,500 Superbirds in order to comply with NASCAR's new rules for racing in 1970. One of the problems Plymouth faced was that these Superbirds had to be completed before January 1, 1970, when new federal headlight laws would go into effect. The Superbird, as designed, would not meet these new federal regulations.

Initially, it was thought that most of the Dodge Daytona's components would simply bolt on to the 1970 Road Runner, thus eliminating development time and solving the headlight problem, but that was not the case. Simply tacking the Daytona's components to a Road Runner to create a Superbird was out of the question. The bodies were not the same and there would be multiple mismatches. Creative Industries was charged with the task of creating the components for a second winged car.

Plymouth's design staff pointed out that with more cars scheduled for production (1,920 were projected by marketing), more attention had to be paid to styling. Also, because of the increased number of cars, production would occur at Chrysler's Lynch Road plant. From there, the cars would be trucked five miles to Chrysler's Clairponte preproduction facility, where the nose and wing assemblies would be installed.

The Superbird's nose, while similar in design to that of the Daytona, was unique. The only interchangeable parts were some of the inner structure and headlight doors. To aid in the transition to the Superbird's pointed nose, Coronet fenders and a modified Coronet hood were added. The center peak of the hood was extended onto the nose. Creative Industries provided the entire front-end assembly, including headlights, to the assembly plant. All that was required was paint.

The rear wing stabilizers were slightly larger at the base and were given a steeper, rearward rake. All Superbirds were equipped with a vinyl roof because of the unique Superbird roof. A special rear window cap was added to the Road Runner's roof to smooth out the roofline. To reduce the cost of expensive metal finishing due to the unique rear window and C-pillars, a vinyl top was specified. This vinyl top hid the joint of the cap to the roof. Because of the metal finishing required, producing a car with a vinyl roof is less expensive than producing one with a painted roof, a little-known fact.

The Superbird also received the smooth A-pillar trim and reversed scoops for the front fenders. Due to certain design compromises with the rear window and nose height, the Superbird's aerodynamics were not as good as those of the Charger Daytona.

The standard engine used for the 1970 Superbird was a 440-ci engine with a single four-barrel carburetor, rated at 375 horsepower. A 390-horsepower 440 with the six-barrel configuration of three two-barrel Holleys was optional along with the Hemi. There were only 135 Hemi Superbirds produced. Unlike a standard 1970

The Superbird's rear wing is similar to the one on the Dodge Daytona. Its high location was for trunk lid opening clearance. The vertical support structures are unique to the Superbird, and they are angled more to the rear than the ones on the Daytona.

Road Runner equipped with a Hemi, the Hemi-equipped Superbird did not have an Air Grabber hood. In addition, there were no external badges for the engine. Like the Daytona, air conditioning was not available, and because of the unique rear window, a rear window defroster and rear seat speaker also were not available on the Superbird. Required options included hood pins, the performance axle package, power steering, and power disc brakes.

The selection for an interior on the Superbird was limited to either an all-vinyl interior in black, or one in white with black trim; but all came with a black headliner. A bench seat was standard and front bucket seats were optional. The interior door trim panels and instrument panel were the same design as the 1970 Road Runner's. The exterior colors for the Superbird were limited to Alpine White, Petty Blue, Lemon Twist, TorRed, Burnt Orange Metallic, Vitamin C Orange, Limelight, and Blue Fire Metallic.

The Superbird's graphics flaunted Plymouth's racing culture. On the quarter panel was a large decal that spelled the word "Plymouth," using the same size and font as the lettering on Richard Petty's race car. The rowdy little bird with a racing helmet tucked under his right wing was on the wing uprights. He was encircled by text that read, "Road Runner Superbird." The headlight doors were blacked out and the driver's side also featured a decal depicting the feisty bird.

Plymouth's marketing and sales departments were confident that the 1970 Plymouth Superbird would sell as quickly as the Dodge Daytona, but it didn't—they had overestimated the market. At a base price of $4,298, it was a tough sell. Many of the 1,935 Superbirds lingered unsold in dealerships. Stories abound of dealers stripping off the special Superbird components and selling the cars as regular Road Runners just to clear them out of the inventory. For the record, First Avenue Plymouth, in Cedar Rapids, Iowa, sold the most of any dealer—15.

Another chapter in the story of winged cars was about to be written with the release of the new 1971 Dodge and Plymouth. Aerodynamic testing of the new models began in January 1970. The additions to the slick new Charger and Road Runner body included a new nose and a raised wing, but the program was doomed. Chrysler slashed its racing budget and NASCAR ruled that all winged cars could only run an engine with a maximum displacement of 305 cubic inches.

Winged cars were also out of step with the average racing fan who was looking for a new car. While everyone wanted to feel like Richard Petty or Buddy Baker while driving their new Chrysler product to the supermarket, they didn't want to be driven to the poorhouse by the effort to buy such an exotic and impractical car. Automobile manufacturers survive on bread-and-butter sedans sold to average citizens, not on the sales of exotic race cars purchased by only a few consumers. The rare, powerful, and exotic Dodge Daytona and Plymouth Superbird made history and are two of the most sought-after muscle cars today.

HEMI 'CUDAS AND CHALLENGERS

1970–1971

On April 17, 1964, Ford Motor Company's Lee Iacocca drove a stake so hard into the ground, it shook the automotive world. Iacocca marked territory and declared Ford as the inventor of the pony car. Up until that time, Ford and its competitors had marketed small cars, but none had the presence and flair of the 1964 Mustang. Everyone was taken by surprise, and many industry experts felt certain that the new Mustang wouldn't sell. Within a few months, however, demand outpaced supply and Chrysler began scrambling to figure out what could be built to compete against the Mustang. Plymouth's first Barracuda was introduced shortly before the Mustang, but it was quickly overshadowed by the wave of enthusiasm created by the new Mustang.

Chrysler had been aware that Ford had been working on a new car based on the Falcon platform. In an attempt to match the upcoming new Ford, Chrysler began work on its own version of a new car intended to appeal to the emerging youth market. This new car would be based on the Valiant platform. Unfortunately, Chrysler's designers and engineers were on a tight budget and were forced to use more of the Valiant than they had planned. The single extravagance they allowed themselves was an expansive rear

When they were released in 1970, Chrysler's new E-body cars were stunning. The styling was exceptionally clean, and the engine selection ran the gamut from a six-cylinder economy engine to the powerful 425-horsepower Hemi. The long option list gave the buyer many different ways to personalize his or her car. In addition to a Hemi engine, this 1970 Dodge Challenger R/T has the SE option, which included a special vinyl top, leather bucket seats, and an overhead console. The Challenger R/T buyer had the choice of longitudinal stripes (like the ones on this car), Bumblebee stripes, or no stripes at all. ©Dale Amy

Above
The new E-body Challenger and Barracuda followed the long nose/short deck design theme that was the accepted standard design philosophy during the pony car era. The taillight panel on all 'Cudas was painted flat black.

Right
The 1970 'Cuda was 5 inches wider and 2 inches lower than the previous Barracuda. The horizontal design of the argent-colored grille added to the perception of the car's width. The underbumper lights are the optional Road Lights that were standard with the 'Cuda. The ELEPHT license plate refers to the nickname of the Hemi engine—Elephant.

With only 14 vehicles built, the 1970 Hemi 'Cuda convertible is one of today's most highly sought-after muscle cars. The new 1970 E-bodies came only in notchback and convertible body styles.

window. At 2,070 square inches, it was the largest piece of glass ever installed in a passenger car.

While Ford's Mustang featured a long nose/short rear deck, Chrysler's new fastback Barracuda was more traditionally proportioned. There were very few changes made to the exterior of the 1965 Barracuda, although Chrysler made some modifications to the 273 engine to increase the horsepower. The 1966 Barracuda received a minor facelift, but offered the same engine lineup used for 1965 models. The largest engine available in 1964 was a 273-ci V-8. Sales of the 1964 Barracuda were only 20 percent of the total Mustang sales.

Chrysler's designers found that they had to offer more than one body style in 1967 to compete against the Mustang's coupe, fastback, and convertible models. The competition would soon be stiffer than ever because there was an underground current of rumors stating that Chevrolet was working on a new pony car, codenamed Panther.

Plymouth's engineers knew that to be competitive, they would have to make room for engines larger than the 273. In the fall of 1966, Plymouth introduced its all-new 1967 Barracuda in three body styles: fastback, coupe, and convertible. The 1967 Barracuda had a more muscular look; it was longer, wider, and lower than the previous model. It also had the 383-ci engine as an available option with a four-speed or TorqueFlite transmission.

Although the width of the engine compartment had been increased by 2 inches, the 383 was still a tight fit. The new sheet metal was placed over the original platform, and reduced the space

Hockey-stick stripes were standard on the 1970 'Cuda. They terminated with a call-out that identified the engine's cubic-inch displacement, or, in the case of the Hemi, the letters "H-E-M-I." The bright color on this Hemi 'Cuda is Panther Pink, a rarely seen shade from Plymouth's exceptional 1970 color palette. ©David Newhardt

Standard on the Hemi 'Cuda and optional on Hemi-equipped Challengers was the Shaker Hood scoop. It was a combination air cleaner and hood scoop. A lever under the instrument panel was connected by a cable that, when actuated, opened a door in the front of the scoop. The most common colors for the Shaker Hood scoop were flat black and argent silver. Certain body colors were also allowed. NASCAR-style hood pins were also standard on the 'Cuda.

Left
Available with certain body colors on the 1970 'Cuda were Elastomeric front bumpers. The only Elastomeric rear bumper available was in Rallye Red. In addition to the Elastomeric front bumper, this Ivy Green Hemi 'Cuda is equipped with the optional Rallye wheels and is a stripe-delete car.

available to accommodate a larger engine. These restricted engine-compartment dimensions prevented the installation of larger engines when the Barracuda was reskinned in 1968. The only exceptions were the specially modified drag race Hemi Barracudas.

In 1967, work began at Chrysler on what would eventually be the 1970 Plymouth Barracuda. In the early stages of the program, only a Barracuda was planned. The Dodge Challenger was not part of the program at that time. Stylists worked with engineering groups to design a car with an engine compartment large enough to accommodate a Hemi or a 440 with air conditioning. The 1960s-era pony car styling trend dictated that a long hood and short rear deck were beneficial in the new design. The long hood would provide plenty of space for Chrysler's premier muscle car engines. The Hemi and 440 engines were popular and the design

Right
Sitting on top of the Hemi engine in this Plum Crazy–colored 1970 Dodge Challenger is a Shaker Hood scoop. It cost an additional $97.30 and was only available with the 440 or Hemi engine.

Below
While similar in body structure to the Plymouth Barracuda, the Dodge Challenger's exterior sheet metal was quite different. Most unique was the fact that its wheelbase was 2 inches longer than that of the Barracuda. It also had a different roof. This 1970 Challenger has the SE option, which included a vinyl roof and a smaller rear window than the standard Challenger. The rear wing, only available in flat black, was also optional.

The 1971 'Cuda received very few changes from the 1970 model. Most notable were the front fender "gills." High-impact paint colors, such as this Sassy Grass Green, were an additional $13.85. Vinyl tops were available in black, white, green, or gold.

parameters were written to include both engines in the packaging of Chrysler's next generation of pony cars.

Instead of building a car from a current vehicle in Chrysler's inventory, it was decided to create an all-new platform—the E-body. The cowl structure was borrowed from the B-body. The cowl is a large and structurally important component in automotive design. By using this large and complex structure, Chrysler saved a great deal of money and engineering work. It also made the adaptation of existing heating and air-conditioning components much easier. Also, by using the B-body's front subframe and rear axle, even more time and money were saved.

With these hard points decided upon, the project was given to Chrysler's Advanced Styling Group. It was their job to package

the vehicle. This included broad-brush drawings that showed the car's major components in place. These drawings were done to determine seating positions, wheelbase, beltlines, and greenhouse. The finalized package drawings were given to the Plymouth studio in order to create the Barracuda's exterior.

With the package work completed, Dodge's product planners felt they would be missing an opportunity by not bringing out a pony car of their own. Using the Barracuda's basic package, they created the Challenger. It was designed to compete in an upscale pony car market against the Mercury XR7 and the Pontiac Firebird. Even though both of Chrysler's new pony cars looked alike, they were actually quite different. The Challenger had a 110-inch wheelbase that was 2 inches longer than the Barracuda's. Both of the cars were low and wide. The new E-body was 2 inches lower and 5 inches wider than the previous Barracuda; the Challenger was 1-1/2 inches wider than the Barracuda.

A decision was made to shelve the fastback body style and concentrate on the coupe and convertible. The design theme for

Plymouth added quad headlights on the 1971 Barracuda and a new body-color grille that has been affectionately called the "cheese grater" for obvious reasons. The addition of the extra headlight required the turn signal to be moved down to the front valance panel.

both cars was a long, low, front end with an aggressively kicked-up rear deck. Designer John Herlitz was responsible for the Barracuda's exterior.

Detroit's auto stylists are passionate about the designs they create. Because most of the studio work is focused on the company's bread-and-butter cars, creative designers often feel unchallenged. Whenever the opportunity comes along to work on something as special as a new Barracuda, designers latch onto such a project like a pit bull on a mailman's leg.

Herlitz credits fellow stylist Neil Walling for the Barracuda's front-end treatment. To accomplish the look they wanted, the hood was stretched and the passenger compartment was moved rearward by 1 foot. By holding the wheelbase at 108 inches, this design resulted in a very short rear deck and small luggage compartment.

When automobiles are in the preproduction phase, a design study called a "luggage stack" is performed. On paper, a studio engineer places standard-sized luggage in the new car's trunk. The size requirement for the new E-body was to only accommodate a set of golf clubs. Luggage space was not going to emerge as a concern for their target market. Because Chrysler knew that the Mustang and Camaro were going to be tough to beat, the E-body's styling had to be the best ever, and this new styling didn't allow much space for luggage.

Herlitz characterized his design as "aggressive," especially when viewed from the rear where the high-placed concave rear taillight panel made the roof appear lower. Both cars featured full wheel openings that perfectly matched the 60-series Polyglas tires that would be featured on the muscle car versions. The side profile on the E-bodies was sleek. The Barracuda had a soft character line that swept down the side, while the Challenger's was much more prominent. The sides of the bodies were well rounded and tucked under along the rocker panel, a distinct departure from the slab-sided cars that Chrysler had designed a few years earlier.

All of the major design elements on the front and rear of the new E-bodies were added to accentuate the car's width. The new Barracuda's grille was a long, thin, oval with deep-set, thin

In 1971, Hemi 'Cudas optioned with disc brakes were equipped with wide Goodyear Polyglas F60-15 tires mounted on body-color steel wheels with dog-dish hub caps. An optional trim ring was available to dress up these wheels, or an optional 15-inch Rallye Wheel could be specified. All 'Cudas with 15-inch wheels were required to add the collapsible spare tire option.

The rear window louvers on this 1971 Hemi 'Cuda are an aftermarket item similar to the factory version offered in 1971. Rear window louvers were available as an option, but required a vinyl top. The rear wing is an original piece, as are the small front spoilers, one of which can be seen on the lower edge of the front fender. This car also has the front and rear body-color Elastomeric bumpers.

horizontal bars featuring a narrow vertical center split. Two large headlights were at the outboard ends. The turn signals were hidden in the upper edge of the grille. Below the thin front bumper was an opening in the front valance panel that allowed additional air to enter the radiator. The Challenger's mesh grille was deep-set and accented by quad headlights. It also had a thin front bumper with a valance panel below. The Challenger's round turn signal lights were neatly tunneled into the front valance panel.

In keeping with good automotive design, the layout of the rear of the new E-body was harmonious with the front end. Both models used thin rear bumpers with a lower valance panel. The ends of the bumpers swept up slightly to blend with the outline of the rear taillight panels. Both cars had small bumper guards on the outboard ends of the bumper. In addition to working as bumper protectors, these guards also cleverly disguised the aft rear spring mounts. Depending on which engine was ordered, rectangular dual-exhaust outlets were formed into the rear valance panel on both cars.

The taillight treatment differed on the new E-body cars. The Barracuda's mildly recessed rear panel housed the license plate in the center and the taillights at the outboard ends. On the 'Cuda this panel was painted flat black, outlined with a thin molding, and had a "'Cuda" emblem on the right side. Each rear light was split into three segments by thin horizontal bars. A backup light

Leather bucket seats could be ordered on a 1971 'Cuda in either tan or black. The second seat-belt buckle on the front seat is for the shoulder harness. This 'Cuda is also optioned with a center console.

was incorporated into the inboard side of each taillight. Because of the thin rear edge of the deck lid and the center-mounted license plate, the Barracuda's deck lid lock was offset to the right. The Challenger used two long, narrow taillight fixtures that were recessed into the rear of the car. Between the two lights was the backup light that had "Dodge" spelled out across the clear lens. The position of this light required the license plate to be mounted on the lower valance panel.

Both cars offered the best Detroit had to offer in the latest design trends and technological developments. One of these technological developments that greatly enhanced the new E-body's appearance was the use of curved side glass instead of flat glass. Curved side glass allowed stylists to pursue body designs that were less boxy.

Flush door handles were a late 1960s development. On the E-body, the lock cylinder was incorporated into the handle's bezel. Hidden windshield wipers were achieved by extending the rear of the hood over the cowl. To provide the needed air for interior ventilation, the rear of the hood had two sets of small slits near the rear edge. One piece of ventless door glass provided a clean side view and lowered production and engineering costs by eliminating the vent window. The sum of all these features, along with Chrysler's artfully crafted styling, produced a vehicle that was on the leading edge of automotive design.

During the design process, Plymouth's designers were intrigued by the 1968 GTO's full urethane front bumper and wanted to incorporate it into the new Barracuda. Cost constraints prevented its inclusion into the design. What they were able to add, however, was an Elastomer bumper option. To create this bumper, Plymouth took an unchromed bumper and molded colored high-density urethane foam over the surface. This could be ordered as a front bumper only or for the front and rear. There were eight available colors that were keyed to the car's exterior paint. In 1970, this option was only available on the Barracuda.

Chrysler knew it had to make its new pony cars available to a wide audience. Each model was offered in several series, with a wide availability of engines and options. This was similar to the successful marketing strategy used by Ford to market the Mustang. Chevrolet followed suit with the Camaro.

In order to meet the needs of every buyer, a wide variety of basic packages were offered for both the Barracuda and Challenger. There were three different series in the Barracuda line: the Barracuda, Gran Coupe, and the 'Cuda. The least expensive was the Barracuda. It was available in both coupe and convertible models with either a six-cylinder or small V-8 engine. The Gran Coupe was the upgraded Barracuda model and it was also available with a six-cylinder or V-8 engine in either coupe or convertible. The 'Cuda was the performance model, and was also available as a coupe or convertible. In keeping with its performance image, the 'Cuda came standard with a 275-horsepower, 340-ci engine and offered optional 383, 440, and 426 Hemi engines.

There was also a special AAR 'Cuda that was offered only as a coupe. It was built to meet the SCCA requirements for Trans-Am racing. The only engine available in the AAR 'Cuda was the six-barrel 340, rated at 290 horsepower.

The Challenger also had two series: the base Challenger with either a six-cylinder engine or a V-8; and the performance R/T (Road and Track), which was only available with a V-8. Both the Challenger and R/T coupe models could be upgraded with the SE (Special Edition) option that included a padded vinyl top and a smaller rear window. The R/T's performance engine list matched that of the 'Cuda. Dodge also had its Trans-Am racer in the Challenger T/A.

Plymouth's 'Cuda E-body was easily identified by its special simulated twin-scoop hood, hood pins, driving lights, Rallye wheels with F70x14-inch white-letter tires, and flat black taillight panel. The optional "hockey stick" body stripe was available only on the 'Cuda. It was listed as a "Sport Stripe" and cost an additional $25.90. This stripe began at the door handle, ran rearward along the top of the quarter panel, and turned downward at the taillight. In prominent letters at the end of the stripe were "340," "383," "440," or "Hemi" to indicate the engine with which the car was equipped. These stripes came only in black, even on black cars.

A special Power Bulge hood was standard on the Challenger R/T. It had a pair of simulated air inlets and hood pins, and was available with a special blackout paint treatment. The R/T also featured F70x14-inch white-letter tires on Rallye Wheels. Challenger R/Ts came

THE COMPETITION

The world of big-block pony cars was rather small in the early 1970s. In 1969, Ford released its Boss 429 Mustang. It was a limited-production run of specially built fastbacks with the new Ford semi-Hemi engine. These cars were designed to provide NASCAR with the required number of production cars to make the Boss 429 engine legal for racing. The Boss 429 cars were built by Car Craft, a Dearborn-area fabrication shop. In 1969, there were 858 Boss 429s built, and in 1970 there were 489. In 1970, the price of a Boss 429 Mustang was $4,932.

In the late 1960s, General Motors restricted its pony cars to engines with a displacement of less than 400 cubic inches. Unlike a Hemi 'Cuda or Challenger, the only way to get a 427-ci engine (430-horsepower ZL-1 or 425-horsepower L72) in a Camaro was with a special COPO (Central Office Production Order) form. This allowed a deviation from Chevrolet's normal production standards. The COPO ordering process was one of those arrangements that was done with a "wink and a nod" to an on-the-ball salesman. Most dealers did not want to bother ordering a car that would be tough to sell in case the person who placed the original order backed out. The ZL-1 option alone cost $4,160. Therefore, there were fewer than 300 COPO 427 Camaros ordered.

In the rarefied air of the big-block pony car, the Plymouth Hemi 'Cuda and Dodge Challenger were breathing pure oxygen. It didn't take a special-order form or a small fortune for the Hemi option. For a 1970 'Cuda, the Hemi option cost $871.45. The exceptionally rare and costly ZL-1 Camaro was indeed faster than the Hemi, but the Boss 429 Mustang was a performance disappointment.

standard with rear Bumblebee stripes. These stripes were painted in white, black, bright red, bright blue, or green, depending on the exterior color choice. A full-length body stripe was offered as a no-cost option on the R/T. The side body stripe accented the Challenger's side character line and was available in white, black, blue, green, or red. Late-year additions to the side stripe included light green and magenta. The rear Bumblebee stripes could be deleted, if desired.

When ordered with the Hemi engine, the 'Cuda came standard with the Shaker Hood scoop. This scoop not only provided fresh air to the Hemi's dual quads, but also scored points with the young, drive-in restaurant crowd. The scoop protruded through an opening in the hood and rocked and rolled while the engine idled. The Shaker Hood was opened by pulling a lever on the instrument panel. The Shaker Hood scoop was a $97.30 option on Hemi-equipped Challenger R/Ts. On both the 'Cuda and Challenger, the Shaker Hood was painted argent silver or flat black; a few were painted in body color. The Shaker Hood was also an option on the 'Cuda and Challenger when any four-barrel–equipped engine was specified. Truth be told, the visual impact of the Shaker Hood was probably more important to most owners than the cold air that flowed to the carbs. When equipped with a Hemi engine, the side of the scoop on the Challenger had a "426 Hemi" emblem, and the 'Cuda's scoop had a "HemiCuda" emblem.

The colors Chrysler selected for the exterior of the new Barracuda and Challenger looked as though they had been lifted from pop artist Peter Max's palette. In the late 1960s, tie-dyed fabrics, bold prints, and bright, vivid colors were popular in fashion and design. In a stroke of brilliance, one of the bright, automotive marketing types added some spice to the names of many of the exterior colors offered. Orange was no longer *orange*—it was Hemi Orange. Yellow became Lemon Twist, purple became Plum Crazy, and light green became Sublime. The boldest color with the most creative name has to be Panther Pink, no doubt owing its name to the *Pink Panther* movies of the era.

While the exteriors of the Barracudas and Challengers were bathed in the trendiest colors with the slickest stripes, the interiors were more conservative. For 1970 models, all E-bodies featured a high-back seat, the result of federally mandated headrests. Standard in the Barracuda was a split-back bench seat with a folding armrest. Bucket seats were standard in all convertibles and the Gran Coupe, and were optional on all other models. Only the base-model Challenger coupe came standard with a split-bench seat. All convertibles and all R/Ts were fitted with bucket seats.

When the SE option was ordered, the bucket seats were covered in leather. All rear seats were bench style and matched the front seat's pattern. A center console was optional. The door and quarter trim panels were a one-piece, formed plastic shell with an integral armrest. 'Cuda models had a "'Cuda" emblem on the front edge of the door panel, and the Challenger's highly detailed door panel had a trim plate with Dodge's tristar medallion in the center of the panel.

The Barracuda and Challenger shared the same coved instrument panel with four large round instrument housings and a standard tachometer. In 1970, federal laws required an energy-absorbing steering column and Chrysler's E-body version looked as though it were a last-minute fix instead of a well-engineered safety device. At the base of the steering wheel was a large-diameter convoluted cylinder to absorb energy.

The standard seat in a 'Cuda was a high-back bench with a fold-down center armrest. A console was not available with this seat, and when a TorqueFlite was selected, the shifter was on the column.

Plymouth produced the ultimate in body stripes with the 1971 'Cuda's billboard stripes. They covered the entire quarter panel and half of the door. The call-out on the door varied with the engine. The call-out for 340, 383, and 440 engines were those numbers, while the one for the Hemi was simply "Hemi." These stripes were only available in white or flat black.

Young people who were buying cars in 1970 wanted a lot of options. Mustang set the trend for a low-cost pony car with a long list of options, and Chevrolet's Camaro foll-owed suit. It was only natural that Chrysler's new E-bodies would have a long list of available equipment to perso-nalize each car to the owner's taste. E-body buyers were able to add an AM/FM stereo radio with a tape player, rear window defogger, rear wing and front spoilers, and a rear window louver package.

Included on the long list of options were five V-8 engines with horsepower ranging from 230 to 425. The Hemi added $871.45 to the price of the 'Cuda and $778.75 to the Challenger R/T. When a Hemi was specified, many heavy-duty components were included. Required with the Hemi engine (and the 440-ci engine) with a four-speed transmission was the Track Pack, option code A33. It included the Super Grip Dana rear axle with 3.54 gears and the heavy-duty cooling system. The alternative Super Track Pack (A34) included the same equipment as the Track Pack option, but offered the 4.10 gears and added front disc brakes. Only two transmissions were offered with the Hemi option: the TorqueFlite and Hurst shifter four-speed manual. The Hurst shifter was unusual because the shift handle didn't use a ball at the end, but a vertical handle called a "strip-grip." Today, this type of shifter is known as the "pistol grip." All Hemi Barracudas and Challengers rode on 15x7-inch wheels mounting F60x15-inch tires. The space saver spare tire was required with the 15-inch wheels.

The 1970 Barracudas were popular, especially with the perform-ance set. There were 1,784 sold with the 440 Six-Pack engine, and 666 sold with the Hemi engine (14 in convertibles and 652 in coupes). The only Chrysler car to outsell the Barracuda in street Hemi versions was the 1968 (Hemi-equipped) Road Runner with 1,011 sold. In 1970, 356 Hemi-powered Challenger R/Ts were produced (9 convert-ibles and 355 coupes). More good news for Chrysler: the 1970 Challenger outsold its closest competitor, the Mercury Cougar.

Minor, but distinctive, changes were made to the 1971 Barracudas and Challengers. The Barracuda's grille was restyled by adding four additional vertical bars into what is commonly called a "cheese grater" grille. This new grille was either painted argent silver

'Cudas could be ordered with two-tone paint, such as this white-over-black version. This is one of 108 Hemi equipped 'Cuda hardtops built in 1971. There were also 7 Hemi 'Cuda convertibles built in 1971. This was the last year for a Barracuda convertible, and the last year for the street Hemi.

with chrome bumpers or body color if the car was equipped with the Elastomer bumper option. The 1970 Barracuda's two large headlights were replaced with quad lamps. "Gills" were added to the 'Cuda's front fender. Thin chrome wheel lip moldings were added and the taillights were revised. The 'Cuda's hockey sticks were replaced with the largest set of stripes ever to decorate a muscle car. They were called "billboard" stripes and covered the entire quarter panel and almost half of the door. The leading edge of the stripe on the door called out the engine's cubic-inch displacement, except for the Hemi, where it spelled out "Hemi." These stripes were only available in black or white.

Minor changes were made to the 1971 Challenger's grille. The full-width inset chrome rectangle was divided in the center into two smaller rectangles. In the rear, the full-width taillight assembly was split into two distinct lamps where the backup light was integrated. The R/T hardtop

received a new set of body side stripes and a pair of simulated brake scoops on each side. For 1971, the R/T convertible was discontinued.

Production numbers for both E-bodies declined in 1971. The total production for all versions of the Barracuda totaled only 16,159, compared to 50,627 in 1970. Hemi 'Cuda production for 1971 broke down to 108 hardtops and only 7 convertibles. Challenger sales were down to just under 23,000 units, with only 71 Hemis.

When the 1972 Challenger and Barracuda were introduced, the Hemi engine was no longer one of the options. It would have been too expensive to make it emissions legal and limited the Hemi engine's performance beyond acceptable limits. The E-body Barracudas and Challengers soldiered on through the beginning of the 1974 model year, when they were canceled in the all-consuming energy crisis.

The legacy the Challenger and Barracuda have left is that of style and performance. With their 1970 introduction, Chrysler took a major leap ahead in automotive design. This was also the peak of the muscle car era. Competition was stiff, and the new E-body had more to offer under the hood than any other pony car available.

HEMI RACE CARS

1964–1971

There were two Chrysler entries at NASCAR's first race at the Charlotte Speedway on June 19, 1949. The results were not spectacular. Chrysler drivers Jimmy Thompson and Frank Smith placed 10th and 21st, respectively. Chrysler's first NASCAR win came later that year when Lee Petty drove his 1949 Plymouth coupe to victory on the half-mile dirt track at Heidelburg Speedway in Pittsburgh, Pennsylvania. In 1949 NASCAR called its top division "Strictly Stock." Petty ended the NASCAR's eight-race season second in points.

NASCAR changed the name of its top division to "Grand National" in 1950, and increased the number of races to 19. Johnny Mantz won the season's premiere race—the Southern 500 held in Darlington, South Carolina, in a Plymouth. Mantz ran the slowest qualifying run in a field of 70 cars with a speed of 73.46 miles per hour. This was 9 miles per hour slower than what the pole sitter, Curtis Turner, ran in his Olds. Mantz not only won the race, but was ahead by nine laps when the checkered flag fell. His average speed for the race was 75.25 miles per hour.

This tortoise-and-hare affair was won purely by strategy. Mantz's Plymouth business coupe was hundreds of pounds lighter than the faster overhead V-8 Cadillacs and Oldsmobiles. Mantz was also crafty enough to fit a set of Firestone Indy race tires onto his car. The other competitors were running street tires, most of which wore down quickly on the asphalt track. Mantz's harder,

Chrysler has a long history of supporting all forms of racing. In 1968, they jumped back into NHRA Super Stock competition with a limited number of specially constructed Dodge Darts and Plymouth Barracudas. These cars were powered by the race Hemi engine and were capable of 130-miles-per-hour speeds in the quarter mile.

when he won seven races in the 1954 season. NASCAR racers of the 1950s were much closer to a showroom model than the cars of the 1960s. Most of the modifications were made to strengthen the body and chassis and a few were made for safety.

Drag racing was rapidly growing in popularity in the mid-1950s. The new overhead V-8s offered more power at a lower cost than the traditional Ford flathead. Drag racers were quick to realize the Hemi's potential and that the fastest of the early dragsters were running Hemis. The burgeoning aftermarket suppliers also jumped on the Hemi bandwagon and provided cams and fuel injectors. Little did they know it was just the tip of the iceberg.

In 1955 and 1956, Carl Kiekhaefer would dominate the NASCAR tracks with his expertly prepared Chrysler 300s. Kiekhaefer brought his money he earned building outboard motors in Wisconsin to the deep South to go racing. With his vast resources, he was able to dominate the season, and with Tim Flock driving, win the NASCAR

Chrysler made a name for itself in the racing world in the mid-1950s with the help of the Hemi engine. This race driver is making a final adjustment on the 331-ci 300-horsepower Hemi in his 1955 Chrysler 300C. In true racer fashion, a little chrome has been added to dress up the engine, and hot rod–style, low-restriction air filters have been added to the dual four-barrel carburetors. *DaimlerChrysler Historical Collection*

compound tires, and lighter, but underpowered car outlasted and outran everyone. Victory lane in 1950 was limited to only three other Chrysler product drivers: Lee Petty, Leon Sales, and Herb Thomas. Herb Thomas would go on to win the 1951 NASCAR title while alternating between a Plymouth and Hudson. In 1952, Lee Petty won three races in his Plymouth.

In 1953, Lee Petty switched to Dodge, due to the 331-ci Hemi engine, which Petty claimed had twice the power of the six-cylinder engines he had been running. Petty ended the season with five victories and garnered second place in the NASCAR standings. Petty was the first to win a NASCAR Championship for Chrysler

Race cars were still being built on Chrysler's regular assembly line in 1964. Here, two workers at the Hamtramck, Michigan, assembly line inspect a lightweight, Hemi-powered Dodge. These cars were built with American magnesium wheels on the front and an aluminum hood that was held down with four pins. They also were built with only two headlights. A grille covers the openings where the inboard lights would normally be placed. *DaimlerChrysler Historical Collection*

Oakland, California's Melrose Motors started racing its *Melrose Missile* Plymouths with the introduction of the Max Wedge in 1962. In 1964, they raced a Max Wedge car and this Hemi, which ran in A/FX. Standing in front of the transporter are Charlie Di Bari, driver Tom Grove, and Jim Di Bari.

Championship. Drivers Speedy Thompson, Norm Nelson, and Fonty Flock were also racing 331-ci Hemis prepared by Kiekhaefer. Lee Petty was able to win six races in 1955, and alternated between a Chrysler and a Dodge. The 1956 season looked like a repeat of 1955 with Kiekhaefer-prepared cars winning 21 of the first 25 races. Buck Baker won the Championship that year driving a Kiekhaefer-prepared Chrysler 300.

In 1956 the Hemi's displacement was increased to 354 cubic inches, and this engine's top rating was 355 horsepower. Unfortunately, one team's complete domination of the series drained the enthusiasm from fans and competitors alike. There was

grumbling in the garage and booing in the stands at the Kiekhaefer entries. Kiekhaefer became disillusioned, and went back to Wisconsin at the end of the 1956 season.

The largest benefactor of Kiekhaefer's racing effort was Chrysler. Although Kiekhaefer, like other racers, was not backed by the factory, Chrysler benefited from the publicity of his racing victories because he used Chrysler's engines. With Kiekhaefer gone in 1957, there were very few Chrysler entries and no wins.

Lee Petty had switched to Oldsmobile and ran one in 1958 when he won the Championship. He started the 1959 season in an Olds, but eventually switched to a Plymouth. Lee Petty would go on to win his third NASCAR Championship that year. Two other notable events occurred in 1959: Richard Petty ran his first NASCAR race and the Daytona International Speedway opened its doors.

Drag racing fever hit Detroit big time in 1959 when it was announced that the NHRA's U.S. Nationals would be held at Detroit Dragway. The Ramchargers, a local club, decided to build a

Left

Dealers were smart enough to take advantage of the race cars that Chrysler was building. They began to feature these cars as part of their regular inventory, and offered both sales and service. Mr. Norm's Grand Spaulding Dodge was a Chicago-area dealer that sponsored its own race cars and kept its showroom stocked with high-performance cars.

Below

Chrysler always built cars within the framework of the rules of the sanctioning bodies. This 1965 Plymouth is also known as an A-990. This was the code for the cars that used lightweight bodies and the race Hemi engine and were built for NHRA Super Stock racing.

car for competition in the Altered class. This class offered very few restrictions to the group's engineering creativity. An old, 354-ci Hemi engine was found, and a 1949 Plymouth business coupe was purchased for $50. The *"High & Mighty"* was one of the most unusual cars to run in the C/Altered class. The entire car was raised higher than any other race car of its day. The club's theory was that the raised position of the body would allow the car's weight to be transferred to the rear wheels to improve traction.

The engine was equipped with dual quads on a fabricated ram intake, and the exhaust headers consisted of megaphone-tipped straight pipes that exited through the fender above the front tire.

Under the hood of the 1965 Plymouth A-990 is a special race Hemi engine. It featured new aluminum heads, oil pump, and water pump. A cross-ram magnesium intake manifold was added to reduce weight.

The top was chopped and the rear fenders had been removed. The team's creativity and engineering skill garnered several track records as well as a change to the NHRA rulebook that dictated maximums in the distance from the track surface to the crankshaft centerline. In 1961, the car was retired after the engine dropped a valve, and the team approached Dodge about help with Super Stock racing.

Lee and Richard Petty both successfully competed in Plymouths in 1960. Richard got his first win and finished second in points to Rex White, who drove a Chevy. Lee Petty's Plymouth also ran well, and carried him to seventh place in the points race. Richard Petty won twice in 1961. Unfortunately, his father Lee's career ended that year with a serious crash at Daytona.

In 1962, Chrysler was heavily involved with drag racing and NASCAR with their introduction of the new 413 wedge engine. Petty garnered eight wins and ended up second in points. Even though they were released in minimal numbers, the new cross-ram–equipped 413 Max Wedge made a big impression on Super Stock racers.

In 1963, the Max Wedge displacement was increased to 426 cubic inches. The lightweight Max Wedge cars were the most potent and plentiful in the stock car ranks at the drag strip. On the NASCAR trail, Petty drove his Plymouth to 14 wins and ended up second in points. This was also a year that saw an amazing level of factory support from manufacturers at the beginning of the year. Chevrolet surprised everyone with an all-new 427-ci engine that dominated the Daytona qualifying round. Unfortunately, General Motors ceased support of all racing efforts soon after the Daytona 500. The gauntlet had been thrown down and Chrysler took up the challenge for the 1964 season.

In 1963, Chrysler management felt it was more important to win NASCAR races than drag races. In the spring of 1963, Chrysler's engineering department was asked what it would take to win the 1964 Daytona 500. The answer was a new Hemi engine. The staff was given the green light and a blank check to complete the project. The only problem was time. They knew the basic head design was good, but they needed to build a block that could withstand the rigors of 500 miles of high-speed racing. The engineers also had to design a valve train capable of sustaining prolonged runs of 6,000 to 7,000 rpm. Testing showed that the blocks had a tendency to crack. A quick fix at the foundry ensured enough blocks for the upcoming race.

Chrysler's first test of a Hemi-powered race car was just weeks before the Daytona race. Paul Goldsmith drove around the Goodyear test track in San Angelo, Texas, at speeds of 180 miles per hour. Engines were shipped to the race teams so they could prepare their cars for the prerace inspection on February 4, 1964.

Above

Harry Holton has been racing his A-990 Plymouth since he bought it as a new car in 1965. Today, it races in Super Stock/B Automatic and runs the quarter in the mid-nine-second range. One big difference between 1965 and today is the size of the rear tire that is allowed.

Left

The interior of the A-990 cars was stripped to the bare minimum. There was no rear seat and the small front bucket seats were attached to the floor with lightweight brackets. Heater, radio, armrests, and the passenger's-side sun visor were deleted to reduce weight. This was the first year for a column shift, which replaced the push-buttons. The transmission valve body was modified to allow a different shift pattern to keep overly eager racers from accidentally selecting reverse.

Carburetors on the A-990 race Hemis were twin Holleys. They were fitted with small velocity stacks that fitted against the openings in the hood for the scoop. The round plugs in the top of the manifold provide access for attachment bolts within the manifold plenum.

Chrysler knew these engines were built with original block castings that had been proven to be susceptible to cracking. It was their hope that the engines could get the teams through inspection, testing, and qualifications before they exhibited any failures.

The drivers of the new Hemi-powered race cars were asked to take it easy and not set the world on fire with each lap, especially during practice. Ford representatives would certainly be timing the new Hemi race cars and would object if an engine not yet in production was significantly faster than any of its own. Initially, both the Ford and Chrysler cars were lapping the track during practice in the 170-miles-per-hour range. Ford was happy that the new Chrysler entries weren't too fast, and NASCAR was happy that there was parity between the makes.

The sandbagging stopped on qualifying day when Paul Goldsmith qualified his Hemi Plymouth with a two-lap average of 174.91 miles per hour. Richard Petty's Hemi Plymouth ran the second-best time of 174.42 miles per hour. Hemi-powered cars also ran away with both qualifying races. The first seven cars on the grid would be either a Hemi-powered Dodge or Plymouth. The engineers' fear that the blocks might crack was confirmed in the qualifying races. New, stronger blocks were cast and stress-relieved before machining. Engines were then assembled, dyno-tested, and quickly shipped to the race teams to replace the older, possibly defective Hemis, which they had been running.

With the exception of David Pearson's DNF, the day was a complete success for Chrysler. Richard Petty won the 1964 Daytona 500 at a record-setting pace, followed by Jimmy Pardue and Paul Goldsmith. Petty went on to win a total of 9 races that year and won the NASCAR Championship. NASCAR wins for the new Hemi in 1964 totaled 26 out of 62 races.

Chrysler's engineers had been more concerned with winning the 1964 Daytona 500 than any other race. Once the NASCAR

With the release of the street Hemi in 1966, Chrysler was allowed to freely run its Hemi engine in NASCAR competition. This is Jim Paschal's Hemi-powered Belvedere hardtop race car. In 1966, NASCAR racers still used production-based passenger cars as the basis for their race cars. This practice is evidenced in this photo by the appearance of a vent window, sun visor, and an exterior door handle. The factory wheel openings have been altered, with little finesse, to accommodate the larger racing tires. *DaimlerChrysler Historical Collection*

program was well under way, their concentration shifted to a drag strip version of the Hemi. Initial tests within Chrysler were disappointing. The Stage III Max Wedge–equipped cars consistently outran the Hemis. It was a long process of sorting out cams and carburetion to get to a point where the Hemi would be faster. Until Chrysler reached that juncture, they could not release the Hemi for competition.

The new Chrysler Hemi produced a lot of overtime for the engineers at Ford. They one-upped Chrysler with the introduction of the Single-Overhead Cam (SOHC) 427 (see sidebar). NASCAR quickly stepped in to stop the impending engine war and banned both the Chrysler Hemi and Ford SOHC engines.

Chrysler responded to the engine ban by withdrawing its factory teams and by boycotting NASCAR. Ford continued to race against the independent racers who were running Dodges and Plymouths and the few who raced Chevys. With a lack of competition, attendance dropped and track owners begged Chrysler to return. NASCAR relented, and by the end of 1965, Hemis were racing again.

Hemis were also racing again in the Super Stock class in 1965. The Dodges and Plymouths built on the assembly line were coded A-990. NHRA rules dictated that cars designed for Super Stock competition could no longer substitute standard body panels for those of fiberglass or aluminum. Chrysler's engineers came up with a plan to comply with the rules, and still build a lightweight car.

They removed everything from the car that was not required by law—radio, heater, sound deadener, and the right-hand sun visor. Special body panels were built using either thinner sheet stock or by standard panels dipped in acid. All other windows, with the exception of the windshield, were lightweight acrylic. To improve traction, the wheelbase on the A-990 car was shortened from 116 inches to 115 inches on the Plymouth, and from 117 inches to 116 inches on the Dodge.

All A-990 cars had a tan vinyl interior. In the front was a pair of small bucket seats from an A-100 van. These seats were mounted in

Many competitors successfully used the street Hemi in competition, even though Chrysler didn't release a version of the race Hemi for drag racing in 1966. This is Jere Stall's 1966 Belvedere sedan at the 1966 NHRA Nationals. © *Larry Davis*

THE COMPETITION—
FORD 427 CAMMER

In 1964, as Chrysler's new Hemi was grinding up the competition at NASCAR tracks and on drag strips across the nation, Ford's engineering staff was hard at work. Ford, like Chrysler, was bound by the 427 cubic inch limit imposed by both NASCAR and NHRA. Ford's engineers knew that freer-breathing Hemi-style heads were the answer to more power. They developed a head similar to Chrysler's with one exception—they added a single-overhead camshaft. Officially called the Single Overhead Cam (SOHC) 427, this engine was simply called the "Cammer" by Ford enthusiasts.

The Cammer engine used the same high-riser 427-ci block (4.232 bore x 3.784 stroke) that Ford had so much success with during the previous two years. The crank and rods were the same except for the added weight on the crank to offset the new pistons. The Cammer's forged aluminum pistons had a raised roof with flats milled on each side for valve clearance.

Each of the unique hemispherical heads housed a single camshaft. For this new design, Ford's engineers used the experience they had gained with the development of their overhead cam engines that were raced at Indianapolis. Although bulky, the Cammer's new heads were free-breathing and they allowed the engine to rev up to and over 8,000 rpm. A single, 6-foot-long chain drove (at half the crankshaft speed) the single cam on each head. The gear attached to the camshaft had an adjustment feature that allowed for different cam timing settings. Atop each head were two rocker shafts with roller cam followers that actuated the valves without the use of pushrods. The elimination of the traditional valve train allowed the engines to reach the higher-rpm range.

Early tests of a single four-barrel–equipped Cammer on a Ford Motor Company dyno produced horsepower readings of over 600. NASCAR quickly banned the engine and Ford used it exclusively in drag racing. The first A/FX Mustangs equipped with the Cammer used twin Holley four-barrel carbs.

Fuel dragster owners soon saw the Cammer's potential. "Sneaky" Pete Robinson, who also ran a Cammer-powered fuel dragster, was the first to win a major NHRA event with Ford Power. He was responsible for the development of many specialized components for the Cammer. Fuel dragster legends Connie Kalitta and Don Prudhomme both found success behind the throttle of a Cammer. Because of NASCAR's ban, the Cammer never saw production. It was a drag race–only engine that reached legendary status in competition against the Hemi-powered dragsters. Within three years of its introduction, Ford discontinued its support of the Cammer.

a fixed position with lightweight brackets. The A-990 cars had carpeting, but there was no backing or insulation and no rear seat. The armrest was also removed from the front door panels.

The engine that powered the A-990 cars was the 426 Race Hemi, fitted with new aluminum heads. The intake manifold for the A-990s was the same basic design as the one used on the drag cars in 1964, except that now it was made from magnesium rather than aluminum. Only two transmissions were available: a heavy-duty four-speed manual with a Hurst shifter or a TorqueFlite. The TorqueFlite had a modified valve body that required manual shifting using a column shifter with a reversed shift pattern. This made it easier to shift in competition. All A-990s had an 8-3/4 Sure Grip rear end with 4.56 gears.

Large custom tubular headers swept into 3-inch collectors. Tapped off the collectors were exhaust pipes that joined into an individual pipe that ran rearward to a single muffler. This muffler was mounted transversely under the rear bumper to concentrate as much weight as possible over the rear wheels. An exceptionally large battery was mounted in the trunk for traction.

Because the A-990 cars met all of NHRA's new rules for the Super Stock class, they were eligible to compete in their National events. A-990 cars made up the entire Super Stock class at the 1965 NHRA Winternationals. Bill Jenkins won the class with an elapsed time of 11.39 seconds at a speed of 126.05 miles per hour. Many original A-990 Super Stocks were rebuilt into altered-wheelbase cars to compete in match racing.

Match racing in the mid-1960s had few rules and those rules were as well enforced as those governing today's professional wrestling events. Match race philosophy at that time was simply to "run what ya brung." Drivers who won races received more bookings, and therefore, more money. To win races, drivers altered the wheelbase and added fuel injection. Although they were fast, the cars began to look less and less like the showroom products with which the customer could identify. Chrysler even built a few of the radically altered wheelbase cars for select factory racers.

By the end of 1965, Chrysler realized the cars they were racing were beyond the reach of the average fan. In a two-page letter dated November 17, 1965, Dale Reeker of Chrysler's Domestic Special Car Product Planning group outlined the company's 1966 racing goals.

In Reeker's letter to Charlie DiBari of Melrose Motors, Reeker explained that they wanted to expand the company's support of Super Stock racing with the new street Hemi. He also pointed out that the cost of supporting supercharged exhibition cars was too high, especially with the new cars that Mercury was building. "We feel that the expense, the safety implications and lack of identity with the product make these cars a poor buy for Chrysler Corporation. Therefore, what we plan to do is use the 1965 cars,

Left

In 1967 Dodge and Plymouth both built 55 special cars, each designed for drag racing in NHRA's SS/B class. The special code for the Dodge was WO23. The engine was a street Hemi with no special parts or preparation. The body was lightened to allow these cars to run at the minimum allowable weight for the class.

Below

As the license plate states, this is one of the 55 Dodge 440 hardtops built especially for drag racing in 1967. The hood scoop is the same as the one added to the 1965 A-990 Super Stock cars.

Staging at the 1967 U.S. Nationals are two SS/BA Hemi cars. The car in the right lane is one of the Plymouth RO23 factory-built racers. The car in the left lane is a standard GTX. The RO23 cars ran at the minimum weight allowed for the class, while other Hemi cars, including the GTX, were heavier. © *Larry Davis*

improve them where we can, run fuel unblown, and if necessary, pick our races. This means that we may have to refuse to match race blown cars or put the price so high the promoters won't pay it."

Reeker went on to explain that in exchange for running their altered-wheelbase *Melrose Missile* 1965 Plymouth, Chrysler would turn over the title to Melrose Motors, provide parts and machining costs, 10 cents a mile for transportation, and $15 a day for travel expenses.

Chrysler was aware that its drag racing program had gotten out of hand. In an effort to go faster and quicker, they had built Funny Cars. While they were fast, the average customer could not afford to easily purchase or own one. With the impending release

Dick Landy was a factory-sponsored racer. His Dodge sponsorship provided him with the best parts and technical assistance available. Here, he motors through the pits at the 1967 U.S. Nationals in his 1967 Hemi-powered Dodge R/T hardtop. © *Larry Davis*

The Dodge WO23 cars were built without radios or heaters in order to save weight. Most racers added aftermarket gauges under the instrument panel and a tachometer on the steering column.

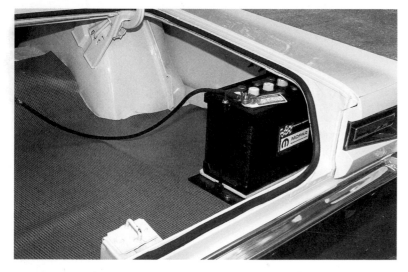

One distinct difference between the WO23 car and a regular-production hardtop was the relocation of the battery to the trunk. This additional weight over the right rear tire aided traction. The WO23 cars did not receive the usual sound-deadening material sprayed on the inside of the body panels.

of the street Hemi, the company would focus its efforts back to showroom-style cars. After all, Chrysler was, first and foremost, in the business of selling cars to the general public.

Dodge focused all of its drag racing efforts on Dick Landy and Plymouth with the Sox and Martin team in 1966. In addition to being excellent representatives for the company, these two high-profile race teams were geographically separated—Landy on the West Coast and Sox and Martin on the East

Coast for more exposure. The new street Hemi made an excellent A/Stock competitor.

In 1966, NASCAR laid down new rules for the Hemi, which included reducing the maximum cubic-inch displacement to 405 cubic inches for Belvederes, Coronets, and the new Dodge Charger. Even with the reduced cubic-inch displacement, Ford wasn't thrilled with the fact that the Chrysler Hemi could run again. Unhappy with the rules, Ford boycotted NASCAR in 1966. David Pearson drove a Dodge and won the season championship. Petty finished third.

In 1967 Richard Petty became "King" when he won 27 of the 48 races he started and set a record by winning 10 straight races. He topped it off by winning the NASCAR crown. Petty admitted years later that during that year, he often backed off of the throttle to keep from embarrassing the competitors. He was also concerned that NASCAR might change the rules if he were any more dominant. Ford eventually returned to NASCAR, but was not competitive.

In 1967 Chrysler once again built a series of cars specifically for drag racing. This time the target was the NHRA's Super Stock B class. To be legal for this class, Chrysler needed to build at least 50 production-line vehicles. To fulfill the requirements, 55 Dodge Coronet 440 hardtops and 55 Plymouth Belvedere II hardtops were built. The Dodges were coded WO23 and the Plymouths were RO23. This special option included a standard production 425-horsepower street Hemi engine and either a column-shifted TorqueFlite transmission with a special 2,300–2,500 stall speed converter, or a Hurst-shifted four-speed with an NHRA-approved explosion-proof bellhousing.

The automatic cars were equipped with a 4.86 Sure Grip 8-3/4 rear end, and the four-speed cars were equipped with the Dana 4.88 Sure Grip, supported by Super Stock rear springs. To reduce the car's weight, the sound deadener, body sealer, front sway bar, radio, and heater were deleted. The battery was relocated to the trunk and a large scoop was added to the hood.

All of these special Dodges and Plymouths were painted white and had black bench-seat interiors. These Hemi cars were capable of running the quarter mile in 11 seconds flat at a speed of 125 and ended up owning NHRA's SS/B class.

Returning for the 1967 season behind the wheel of their Mopars were Dick Landy and the team of Ronnie Sox and Buddy Martin. In addition to racing specially prepared street Hemi– and 440-equipped hardtops, they also held high-performance clinics at selected Dodge and Plymouth dealerships across the country.

These clinics were scheduled to occur three days in advance of an appearance at a local drag strip. At these clinics, racing movies were shown, extensive displays of performance parts were exhibited, and the experts answered technical questions. In addition, a

"Pop Stock Eliminator" event would be held at the strip. A spectator, a member of the media, or a local radio DJ would compete against one of the pros on the track.

The lucky contestant would drive a 440-equipped car against the pro in a Hemi. The amateur was given a handicap start. If the amateur beat the pro, he received a trophy and a prize. Even if the contestant didn't win, he was still awarded a prize. These clinics were designed as promotional events to increase sales of high-performance cars at local Plymouth and Dodge dealerships.

In 1968, Chrysler once again ventured into the world of custom-built Super Stock cars. This time they used the smaller Plymouth Barracuda and Dodge Dart as the starting point for their new factory racers. These cars were the brainchild of Chrysler's Dick Maxwell. Maxwell felt that the powerful Hemi engine in the smaller and lighter A-body Darts and Barracudas would be unbeatable. Unfortunately, there was debate within Chrysler about the value of these cars and getting approval was more difficult than imagined. The saving grace was the steady growth of the muscle car market and the positive press coverage from the success that both Dodge and Plymouth had been experiencing on the drag strip.

Chrysler engineer Bob Tarrozi developed the specifications and built the prototype using a Barracuda platform. Both the Barracuda and Dart were built on the same platform and any modifications made to fit the big Hemi into the Barracuda would be made on the Dart. Because of the width of the engine, the front spring towers had to be reworked and a special brake master cylinder was added.

Tarrozi followed Chrysler's vehicle lightening formula of lightweight fiberglass front fenders and hood. The body panels and bumpers were acid dipped. Deleted from the car's interior were the heater, radio, rear seat, body insulation, and sound-deadening material. Two Dodge van lightweight bucket seats were added, and the windows were made from a lightweight polymer and all the window mechanisms were removed. The quarter windows were fixed and the door glass was raised and lowered with a strap.

The engine selected for these special 1968 Barracudas and Darts was Chrysler's race Hemi engine, which featured 12.5:1 pistons, dual Holley carburetors on a magnesium cross-ram intake manifold, an aluminum water pump, and Hooker exhaust headers. The Hemi Darts and Hemi Barracudas were built with either a TorqueFlite automatic or a four-speed manual transmission.

Once the project was approved, Hurst Corporation's Detroit-area buildshop was contracted to construct 50 Dodge Darts and 50 Plymouth Barracudas. Later, an additional 25 of each car were produced, but some sources claim Hemi Dart production totaled 83. These cars were shipped in primer to the dealers. The fiberglass front clip components were coated with an unpainted gel. None of

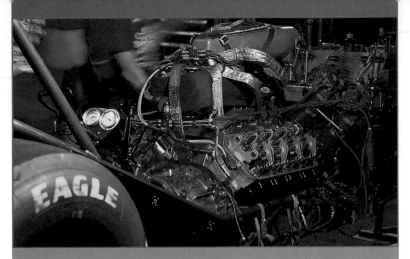

The only engine used in today's Top Fuel and Funny Cars is an all-aluminum version of the Hemi. This Funny Car's Hemi engine is being prepared for the next round of racing. On nitromethane, this engine produces over 6,000 horsepower and can propel a Funny Car to speeds in excess of 300 miles per hour.

NITRO-BURNING HEMIS

Since the beginning of drag racing in the 1950s, the Hemi engine was been the sport's most powerful and prolific engine. Drag racers learned of the Hemi's vast untapped power and proceeded to add cams, blowers, and fuel injection to fully utilize its potential. When nitromethane became the accepted fuel for dragsters, the Hemi's vast breathing ability and strong bottom end made it the standard for those competing in the Top Fuel class.

When the 426 Hemi was first introduced in 1964, competitors were slow to switch. The 392 ci Hemi had been around a long time and the aftermarket was rife with speed equipment. The top engine builders saw the advantages of the new 426 Hemi and were quick to develop it into a winner.

The final phase of development of the Hemi engine for Top Fuel was the manufacture of aluminum aftermarket blocks and heads. In the 1970s, legendary engine builder Keith Black was the first to build an aluminum Hemi block. This gave the Top Fuel dragster builders an engine that was light, strong, and powerful. Since then, several other engine builders have developed new aluminum Hemi blocks for Top Fuel and Funny Car racing. Also in the 1970s, Pro Stock racer Dick Landy developed the Hemi head with two plugs per cylinder. Today, all of the top nitro racers run CNC-machined aluminum billet heads with two plugs per cylinder.

To develop 6,000 horsepower, these engines consume five gallons of nitro per each 4.5-second, quarter-mile run. One of the byproducts of burning nitromethane is oxygen. Therefore, mixtures as high as 1 to 1 can be fed into the cylinders. After each race, these nitro-burning Hemis are torn down and completely rebuilt. Although the rules allow any American-made, two-valve-per-cylinder, 90 degree V-8 to be run in Funny Cars and Top Fuel dragsters, only the Hemi is used.

Left

The engine in the WO23 and RO23 race cars was a production street Hemi engine. The cars were equipped with a larger pulley on the alternator (to reduce horsepower draw) and a positive battery terminal connection on the left front inner fender. The hood's inner support structure was cut away to allow for an aluminum reinforcement for the opening to the scoop.

Right

In 1968, Chrysler was back into Super Stock competition with two of the most audacious cars ever built for drag racing—the Hemi Dart and the Hemi Barracuda. The Hurst Corporation, under contract to Chrysler, built 75 of each. Fittingly, these would be the last cars any manufacturer would ever build specifically for drag racing.

Below

Chrysler engineer Bob Tarrozi used a 1968 Barracuda as the prototype for the A-body race car. In addition to squeezing the large Hemi engine into the small chassis, he worked extensively on decreasing the weight of the car by using fiberglass body panels.

At the 1970 Daytona 500, Ramo Stott, driver of this Plymouth Superbird, placed eighth in both the 125-mile qualifying race and the Daytona 500. The pole sitter was Buddy Baker, who ran a speed of 192.62 miles per hour in his Dodge Daytona. The race winner was Pete Hamilton in a Superbird that was prepared by Richard Petty. *DaimlerChrysler Historical Collection*

these cars met 1968 federal emission laws and could not be legally licensed for the street and were only used for drag racing. These special Barracudas and Darts were the last purpose-built drag racing cars to come out of Chrysler.

Dodge introduced a sleek new Charger for the 1968 season. As good as the car looked, it had a few aerodynamic flaws. The large, open grille and tunnel back window were hindering the car's performance. The fix came about in 1969 in the form of the Charger 500. Its grille was pulled forward, flush with the end of the hood, and a new rear window was added to make the car a true fastback. The Charger 500 was a big improvement over the standard Charger, but it was not as slick as the Ford Torino Talladega. The ultimate solution came midseason with the release of the Charger Daytona.

The Charger Daytona used the roofline of the Charger 500 and added a sleek nosepiece and a large rear wing. Wind tunnel tests were run and the downforce generated by the rear wing provided as much as 600 pounds of stabilizing pressure on the rear wheels. Charlie Glotzbach tested a new Daytona for Chrysler at its Chelsea Proving Grounds and hit speeds as high as 243 miles per hour on the five-mile oval.

The Daytona's debut was to be at the new Talladega Speedway. Many drivers refused to compete because they felt that the track was too fast and that conditions were unsafe. The rough track surface chewed up tires and Firestone withdrew its tires from the race when it discovered the tires would last only four laps at speed.

Charlie Glotzbach was the fastest qualifier in a Dodge Daytona, but declined to compete because of the track. Only two Dodge Daytonas started this race that was, by now, populated primarily by cars and drivers from a lower division. Richard Brickhouse drove his Daytona to the winner's circle. Because of the controversy surrounding the track, the Daytona's debut and first win were inauspicious.

The new Daytona also caused a stir within the Chrysler camp. When Richard Petty got wind of the sleek Daytona, he wanted

Chrysler's winged race cars were also used on road courses. Here, a Road Runner Superbird leads a Dodge Daytona. The left headlight door of the Superbird has been removed and a screen has been placed over the opening to allow airflow to the oil cooler. *DaimlerChrysler Historical Collection*

one. He was informed that he couldn't have one because the new Daytona was a Dodge and he drove a Plymouth. In a fit of anger, he left Plymouth and drove a Ford for the 1969 season.

Plymouth was able to woo Petty back with the 1970 Superbird. With the Superbird, Petty was able to compete and won 18 races in 1970. He split his driving between a Road Runner on the short tracks and a Superbird on the longer, high-speed tracks.

There was also a big change on the drag strips in 1970 when the NHRA introduced Pro StockPro Stock as a new class. Pro Stockers gave drag racing fans a late-model production car with enough improvements to make it faster than a stock version. Since the car's stock design cues remained apparent, it made for good brand wars on the track. The Pro Stock class Pro Stock was a good idea at the time and it prevails today as one of the most fiercely contested classes.

The Pro Stock class gave manufacturers a high-profile series to showcase their latest big-block engines in lightweight bodies. The 7-pounds-per-cubic-inch rule opened the door for Hemi 'Cudas, 427 Camaros, and Cobra Jet Mustangs. The term "stock" was a bit of a misnomer, since this class allowed engine modifications that included tunnel-ram intakes, fiberglass body components, and large hood scoops. To maintain their stock appearance, the cars had to run a stock wheelbase and the rear tires had to fit within the original wheel openings.

Bill Jenkins won the first Pro Stock contest at the 1970 Winternationals with a 1968 Camaro. With such names as "Dyno" Don Nicholson, Dick Landy, and Sox and Martin, the list of drivers read like a Super Stock meet from the early 1960s. In the final round, Jenkins, running a 9.98 elapsed time, defeated Sox and Martin's Hemi 'Cuda, which ran a 10.12. The balance of 1970 was dominated by Sox and Martin's Hemi 'Cuda.

The popularity of the new Pro Stock class was evident at the Super Stock Nationals in York, Pennsylvania, where a 50-car field lined up for eliminations. Ronnie Sox, behind the wheel of Sox and Martin's Hemi 'Cuda, was the eventual winner, and ran a best of 9.86 seconds elapsed time. Ronnie Sox carried a great deal of momentum into the 1971 season; by the end of that season, he had won the majority of the races and held the e.t. record at 9.52 seconds.

Hemi-powered Dodge Challengers and Plymouth 'Cudas were the mainstay of the Pro Stock class, and won 12 of 15 major events. Rule changes in 1972 favored small-block power and required Hemi-powered cars to add ballast. By the end of the 1973 drag racing season, Chrysler moved its support to other Super Stock and bracket classes. They would not return to Pro Stock until the 1990s.

By the end of 1970, NASCAR was determined to make life unpleasant for those who wanted to run a Hemi or a winged car. For 1971, those who chose to run a Hemi (or Ford Boss 429) were required to run a restrictor plate with 1-1/4-inch bores. This effectively choked the Hemi engines out of existence, while the wedge engines ran unrestricted. Winged cars were legislated out of competition by virtue of a rule that allowed the use of engines with a maximum displacement of only 305 cubic inches. In 1973, NASCAR required a special small Holley carburetor on engines displacing over 366 cubic inches. By 1974, all Hemis were retired from NASCAR competition.

Chrysler's Hemi racing heritage in NASCAR and drag racing is as rich as that of the Ferrari in Formula One. The Hemi was the mainstay of the early drag racers and made its mark in the formative days of NASCAR. The release of the new Hemi engine in 1964 revolutionized drag racing and set the NASCAR world spinning. As a testament to the Hemi's staying power, many of the specially built 1965 A-990 Plymouths and 1968 Hemi Darts and Barracudas are still competitive in NHRA today. Records have been written and racing careers made with Hemi power.

Right
When Richard Petty found out about the Dodge Daytonas, he wanted one. When told he drove for Plymouth and not Dodge, he left to drive a Ford. When Petty saw the plans for the new Superbird, he quickly returned to Plymouth. Petty won several races behind the wheel of his Superbird. *DaimlerChrysler Historical Collection*

CHAPTER NINE

HEMI CLONE CARS

1964–1971

Only the greats are imitated. There must be a thousand Elvis impersonators in the world of entertainment. They have copied the look, songs, and experience of the "King of Rock and Roll." They have the slicked-back black hair and sideburns, metal sunglasses, and the sequined white jumpsuit. Their performances have been refined to replicate every hip wiggle and karate kick in Elvis' stage act. In many instances, their singing is as good, or better than the King's. An Elvis impersonator is a great alternative for those who never had a chance to see the real Elvis perform.

The greats in the world of muscle cars also are imitated. Many people remember 1964 and 1965, which were the glory days of Hemi drag racing. It was a time when Hemi-powered Plymouths and Dodges dominated Super Stock and A/FX. Unfortunately, there are only a few of the original factory race cars left. If one can be found, it will be expensive and if properly restored, and won't be driven on a regular basis. The solution for those who want the experience of driving one of the greatest cars ever constructed is to build a clone.

It was during the 1980s that unethical restorers were converting small-block Corvettes into big-block cars and transforming the Pontiac LeMans into a GTO. In some cases, this transformation doubled the value of the car. These cars were relatively easy to convert because there was an abundant supply of the engines needed to make the change.

Anyone who went to the drag strip in the mid-1960s can remember the Hemi Plymouths that dominated the Super Stock and A/FX classes with two-door Savoy sedans that looked like this. Appearances can be deceiving. This is actually a carefully crafted clone built to look like one of those historical drag racers.

The only Hemi cars Plymouth built in 1965 were the A-990 cars, which were specifically designed for drag racing. They were all two-door sedans like these Plymouth clones built by Bob Mosher.

Many unwary buyers were caught up in the thrill of owning a classic muscle car and failed to do their homework, and unknowingly bought a clone. It was often a friend or a stranger at a car show who pointed out the car's inconsistencies. Many times this resulted in lawsuits, not to mention some very angry and embarrassed owners whose love affair for their new muscle car ended abruptly.

One variety of car that was not cloned on a regular basis was the Hemi car. While a Hemi-powered Road Runner or Charger far outpaced the value of a non-Hemi version, cloning one was often too expensive to make the conversion profitable. Hemi engines were a rare and costly find. Also, there were too many observant Mopar enthusiasts who could spot the smallest inconsistency in any restoration, much less a clone car. Once identified as a clone, the suspect Hemi car was banished to a life of shame and the restorer was blacklisted.

By the 1990s, the stigma of owning a clone car had changed. Buyers had become more knowledgeable and those who were cheating the public with fake Corvettes and GTOs were out of business. Also, Hemi engines were becoming more plentiful, and there was a growing interest in the "plain Jane" Super Stock cars that ran in the early and mid-1960s. These were the original muscle cars that fought feverish battles on the drag strips and streets of America.

Dodge and Plymouth Max Wedge cars were first introduced to the Super Stock battles in 1962; by 1963, they were the cars to beat. They were the audacious race cars with a snarling hood scoop and the on-track performance to prove they weren't just drag strip posers.

Chrysler continued its drag strip performance parade with the release of the Hemi in 1964 and the A-990 Super Stock in 1965. With a few exceptions for the altered-wheelbase A/FX racers, most of these cars were two-door sedans. These were the least expensive and the most lightweight cars available. Images of Roger Lindamood's 1964 Hemi-powered Dodge sedan and Grumpy Jenkins' *Black Arrow* A-990 Hemi have driven car builders who want something a little different and fast to build clones of these early Super Stock racers.

Finding an original Hemi race car was next to impossible. Most had been shipped to the junkyard after they had outlived their useful racing days. The bodies had been hacked, cut, and welded in an effort to modify the car for racing. Racing itself also took a toll on the body structure and exterior body panels. If a restorable original Hemi race car were found, it would be very expensive. Also, most people found that driving a rare and expensive Hemi race car on the street was not something a sane person would do.

The only logical alternative was to build a clone car by recreating a 1964 Hemi Plymouth or Dodge or a 1965 Plymouth or Dodge A-990. In 1964 and 1965, Dodge and Plymouth sold thousands of two-door sedans with either a six-cylinder engine or a small V-8.

Joe McCaron is another Southern California clone car builder who built this 1965 Plymouth A-990 clone. In keeping with the mid-1960s drag race look, McCaron used American Mags and added a tach to the top of the instrument panel.

Above

The powerful Hemi engine in Brian Dickie's 1964 Plymouth clone can quickly turn big sticky tires into smoke. In street trim, Dickie took this car down the quarter mile in 11.50 seconds at a speed of 121 miles per hour, the kinds of elapsed times that lightweight A-990 race cars were turning in the mid-1960s.

Right

When building a clone car, the owner has the freedom to make changes. Such changes to an original Hemi car can hurt the value of the vehicle. The objective is to get the look and feel of the original Hemi car. Here a "Hemi" decal has been added to the hood scoop, a full rear seat has been installed, and radial tires have been selected.

The Hemi engine in Brian Dickie's 1964 Plymouth is a new Mopar Parts Hemi block that has been bored to 4.40 inches. A Mopar 5/8-stroker crank brings the total displacement to 510 cubic inches. Mopar aluminum heads and water pump are used along with an original cross-ram intake and Holley carbs. On unleaded gas, this engine develops 635 horsepower at 6,100 rpm, and 600 pounds of torque at 3,500 rpm.

Many of these cars survived, but were rejected by restorers because of their low restoration value.

Many of these pedestrian sedans were eventually crushed into square blocks of steel because of their low market value. Today, these 1964 and 1965 two-door sedans are highly sought after because they can be easily cloned into Hemi race cars of the 1960s.

Someone who has made a successful business out of cloning Hemi cars is Bob Mosher, owner of Mosher's Muscle Cars in Monrovia, California. Mosher grew up in the Los Angeles area and was extremely fond of the Mopar Super Stocks that he saw racing at Lion's Speedway in Long Beach, California, as well as several other area drag strips in the 1960s. Mosher's name might not be familiar, but his life as a child was played out on the *Leave it to Beaver* television series that his father, along with Joe Connelly, developed, wrote, and produced. Today, Mosher has outgrown the trials that plagued "the Beave" and has devoted himself to building and restoring 1961–1965 Max Wedge and Hemi cars. In the past 15 years he's restored several original A-990 cars and has built dozens of 1964 Hemi sedans and 1965 A-990 clones.

Only a few modifications to a B-body are necessary in order to allow the installation of a Hemi engine. First, the right-hand shock tower must be modified for engine clearance. This was originally done at the factory on new Hemi cars and is simply a matter of creating a depression for cylinder head clearance. The non-Hemi K-member must be modified for the Hemi engine; otherwise, special aftermarket engine mounts must be added. Most builders of these early Hemi clone cars also connect the front and rear subframes for extra body rigidity.

Most builders add a set of mini–tubs to the rear wheelhouse to accommodate rear tires up to 10 inches wide. This small change is accomplished by moving the inner half of the rear wheelhouses inboard and adding a 2- or 3-inch-wide filler strip to close the gap. Moving the springs inboard is accomplished with a Mopar spring relocation kit. These changes allow the use of 10-inch-wide rear tires.

One of the benefits of owning a clone car rather than an original is the ability to make changes in handling or appearance. Although the clone cars that Mosher and his contemporaries build are not exact replicas, they still exude the nasty attitude displayed by the originals.

Faithful recreation of the Hemi race car interior completes the clone car package. Dodge A-100 van bucket seats, covered in Champagne-colored vinyl, are mounted in a fixed position on aluminum stanchions and the rear seats are deleted, as well as the radio, heater, door armrests, and the passenger-side sun visor. The battery is mounted in the trunk and a tach is mounted on top of the instrument panel, just like they were in the mid-1960s.

One of the drawbacks to building a Hemi clone car has always been finding an affordable Hemi engine. Today, there are several alternatives. Mopar Performance Parts has prepackaged several Hemi Crate engines. Anyone can walk into their favorite Mopar parts department and order an all-new 426-ci Hemi engine, starting at just under $10,000.

This engine (part number P5249667) is rated at 465 horsepower and 486 foot-pounds of torque. It features a Mopar Performance Parts cast-iron block with cross-bolted mains, cast-iron heads, forged 9:1 pistons, a 278-degree duration cam, and an aluminum dual-plane single four-barrel intake manifold. Chrome valve covers, a water pump, and an electronic distributor are also included.

All that's needed to finish the package are pulleys, fan, ignition wires, carburetor (a 750-cfm Holley is recommended), and exhaust headers (2.0-inch diameter). With this engine's 9:1 compression ratio, it will run on unleaded gas and still develop 40 more horsepower than the original street Hemi engine.

If 465 horsepower is not enough, Mopar Performance Parts offers two other Hemi Crate engines. The first is a stroked version with a hotter cam. A forged crankshaft with a 4.15-inch stroke is added, which increases the displacement to 472 cubic inches, and

Above

Plymouths were popular at the drag strip in the mid-1960s, and are used more often today for clone projects. Dodge also built A-990 cars in 1965, and like this 1965 Dodge sedan built by McCaron, A-990s have occasionally been turned into stunning Hemi clone cars. For safety reasons, most clone car builders install front disc brakes.

Left

The large engine bay on a mid-1960s B-body car, such as this 1965 Dodge, easily accepts a Hemi engine. The only modification needed for engine clearance is to the right shock tower.

Right

In 1965, Chrysler dropped the push-button–controlled TorqueFlite for a more traditional column shift. The race cars had a reversed valve body that allowed for a reversed shift pattern. This reversed pattern prevented the race car driver from accidentally selecting reverse during a race. This unique feature is incorporated into all 1965 A-990 clones.

The Hemi engine, especially one with a cross-ram intake, is an impressive piece of machinery, whether it's in a mid-1960s B-body or on an engine stand. Because there were never any street-type exhaust manifolds made for the early B-bodies, all clone car builders have custom headers built.

Above right

The interiors of the 1964 and 1965 B-body race cars were stripped to the bare minimum, and clone car builders do the same. The bucket seats are from an A-100 van and are mounted in a fixed position on aluminum brackets. There were no armrests on the doors, nor were there radios or heaters on the original race cars; clone builders follow suit. The interior color of this 1965 Dodge is the same champagne color as that found on an original A-990 Dodge.

a 292-degree duration hydraulic camshaft is installed. The compression ratio on this engine is 9:1 and all that is required is a single four-barrel carburetor. This engine produces 525 horsepower at 6,000 rpm and 540 foot-pounds of torque at 3,600 rpm on premium unleaded gas.

The monarch of the Mopar Crate engines is a 528-ci King Kong that produces 610 horsepower. It runs the same camshaft and stroker crank as the 472-ci engine, but is bored .25 of an inch for the extra displacement. This engine has a compression ratio of 10.25:1 and Mopar Parts claims it will run on premium unleaded gas. These engines are the easiest out-of-the-box solutions to create a Hemi car from any early B-body.

Within the last decade, Chrysler has reissued all of the basic parts for those who want to build their own Hemi. Chrysler started to remanufacture components in 1992, as the demand for the Hemi grew. All of the Hemi's tooling had been scrapped years ago, but the original drawings were still on file. A new block was cast with thicker decks for added rigidity. New heads were also cast. With the exception of new accessory mounting bosses on the ends, they look just like the originals, and even have the core plugs in the ends of the heads.

Because of advanced casting technology, these plugs are no longer needed, but were added to preserve the original appearance. These new heads breathe better than the originals and are considerably stronger. Also available at the Mopar parts counter are aluminum Hemi heads. These heads have the same-sized valves and combustion chamber as the cast-iron heads. To discourage the use of these components in a clone, Mopar has cast an "M" after the part number.

Walt Knoch took a 1970 Barracuda convertible that had originally been equipped with a 318 V-8 and converted it into a Hemi 'cuda. The Hemi engine Knoch used wasn't just any Hemi, but an original A-990 race Hemi still in its original crate. His father bought it for $1,000 in early 1965.

Another solution to finding an original Hemi engine is bolting a set of Hemi heads on to a 383–440-ci wedge engine. Chrysler's Hemi heads will not bolt on to this series of engine, but Stage V Engineering in Walnut, California, has developed a set that will bolt on. The heads developed by Stage V are based on those developed for Top Fuel nitro-burners. They are cast from C-355 aluminum and are CNC-machined. C-355 is aerospace-quality aluminum and is 20 percent stronger than an ordinary aftermarket aluminum head cast from 356 alloy. With a 10:1 compression ratio, Stage V's heads are designed for use with premium unleaded gas. They are fully ported, come with hardened valve seats, and bronze-wall valve guides. The heads are designed for a 2.20-inch-diameter intake and 1.90-inch-diameter exhaust valves. They are smaller than a stock Hemi, but are slightly larger than a stock 440 wedge. These heads flow 20 percent better than an original stock Hemi head.

A few changes must be made to a wedge block to accept the Stage V heads. The tapped head bolt attaching holes in the block between the cylinders must be enlarged and tapped for the larger 1/2-inch head bolts required. About 1/8-inch-deep clearance grooves must be cut into the wall of the block in the valley area for

pushrod clearance. Because there is no provision for oil return from the head, an external drain line must be added from the rear of the head to the block. Finally, the engine must be equipped with Hemi-style domed pistons. A complete Stage V Hemi head–equipped wedge engine weighs 125 pounds less than an original Hemi. To round out the early race Hemi look, the cross-ram intake used on all early race Hemis is a direct bolt-on.

While Bob Mosher and his contemporaries have concentrated on the early (1964–1965) B-bodies, few builders have faithfully reproduced 1966–1971- Hemi clones. Unfortunately, with the

1966 and later Hemi cars, the romantic element from the formative days of Super Stock drag racing of charging down the drag strip in a stripped-down sedan no longer exists. The later cars were built in greater numbers and never had the raw edge of the early race Hemis and thus have not been cloned as frequently.

The exception to that rule is the Barracuda- and Challenger-based Hemi clones. These E-body cars are, hands down, the best-styled vehicles to come out of the muscle car era. A Hemi 'Cuda convertible is one of the most rare of the breed, but many Barracuda convertibles were built with a variety of other engines.

When shopping for a 1966–1971 street Hemi, look for some of these unusual construction traits that will help you to differentiate a real factory-built Hemi car from a fake. The fifth digit on the VIN tag defines a Dodge or Plymouth's original engine. The fifth digit on a 1966 Hemi car should read "H"; on a 1967–1969 Hemi car, it should read "J"; and on a 1970–1971 Hemi car, it should read "R."

Another thing to look for under the hood is the method of attachment of the power brake booster. All Hemi cars with power brakes had a booster that could be removed without going under the instrument panel. Removal of the booster allowed easy removal for the left-side valve cover. While Hemi cars never came with air conditioning, they did have all the heavy-duty cooling equipment that was installed on A/C-equipped cars, including the larger 26-inch radiator and heavy-duty radiator support. Hemi cars equipped with power steering came with a unique power steering pump that had a key-slotted shaft and a pulley attached with a nut. This pump also used a wider belt. Most Hemi cars with an automatic transmission had a separate transmission cooler that was mounted in front of the radiator.

More investigation needs to be done under the car in order to know whether you've got a clone car or an original Hemi. All Hemi cars came with torque boxes mounted in front of the rear leaf springs. This box connected the bulkhead to the rocker's side rails for extra strength. It was there to accept and distribute throughout the body structure the extra torque produced by the Hemi engine. All Hemi cars had 11-inch brakes and an additional half leaf in the right rear spring (6 leaves on the left side and 6-1/2 on the right), but it should be noted that 440-equipped cars also had the additional half spring. All four-speed Hemi cars were equipped with the Dana 60 rear end. This rear end was optional on Hemis with automatics and many were so equipped. All Hemi cars, and some 440 cars, were equipped with 3/8-inch fuel lines. The Hemi engine's unique side engine mounts required a special K-member that was only used on Hemi cars. This K-member also had a skid plate to protect the Hemi's deeper 6-quart oil pan. Some 440-equipped cars also had this skid plate.

Between 1966 and 1969, all Hemi engines were equipped with a mechanical camshaft. In 1970 and 1971 all street Hemis used a hydraulic camshaft. All 1969 and later Hemi cars, with the exception of the 1970 Charger, Dodge Daytona, and Plymouth Superbird, had some type of standard, cool-air induction system. Also, a few Hemi Challenger R/Ts were built without the Shaker Hood. All street Hemi engines were painted Hemi Orange, a shade of orange that had more red pigment in it than the race Hemi engine color.

The old adage "look before you leap" has never been more true than when buying a Hemi car. "Original" Hemi cars are one of the most sought-after muscle cars and are also one of the most expensive. When buying one, it's prudent to ask for broadcast sheets (the manufacturer's roadmap for assembly) that are often hidden in the car, window stickers, dealer invoices, or any other documentation the seller may have. Ask as many questions of the owner as you can. Contact Mopar enthusiasts to get the facts if you remain unsure. You can always concede the fact that not everyone can own an original Hemi car and that the alternative might be to build a Hemi clone for yourself.

Building Hemi clone cars has been made infinitely easier by Chrysler's release of Hemi Crate engines. For a little under $10,000, anyone can have a Hemi like this one that produces 465 horsepower on unleaded gas.

CHAPTER TEN

THE NEW HEMI

No one would have ever guessed that Chrysler might one day resurrect the Hemi engine or that 425-horsepower muscle cars would once again be available at the dealerships. But a series of events led Chrysler to design a new V-8 engine and at the same time create an all-new rear-wheel-drive platform perfectly suited for that new engine. As the planets aligned over Detroit, the new Hemi engine was reborn along with the exciting LX platform. Hemi muscle rules the streets again.

Throughout the 1990s, Chrysler and the other major automotive manufacturers had great success selling pickup trucks and sport utility vehicles. The Dodge Ram led the way for Chrysler's full-size pickup efforts. To keep the Ram on the leading edge, a more modern V-8 engine would have to replace its vintage 5.9-liter V-8. The need for a new truck engine would eventually lead to the new Chrysler Hemi engine.

Initially, no one mentioned the word "Hemi" as Chrysler's team of engineers created a list of objectives for the new V-8 engine. They envisioned an engine that would be rugged and simple—no active manifolds and no variable valve timing. Engineers were determined to stay away from too much high-tech gadgetry, things that not only held little appeal for the average truck customer, but that might even risk driving them away from the product. A double-overhead cam all-aluminum engine with four valves per cylinder that revs to 9000 rpm would not work in the Ram truck, nor would it fit the image.

The bold hood graphics on the new Dodge Daytona R/T proudly announces that there's a Hemi engine lurking beneath. The new Hemi engine offers 1960s-era muscle car performance with excellent gas mileage, thanks to MDS (Multiple Displacement System) technology.

Chrysler initially designed the new 5.7-liter Hemi engine for its Ram pickup line of trucks. Truck owners look for power, simplicity, and durability in an engine—all qualities of the new Hemi.

Because this new engine was intended for a truck, Chrysler's engineers determined that a cast-iron block would be more practical than an aluminum block. The block design they developed had some of the same characteristics as the original Hemi, including a deep skirt and a high-mounted camshaft. They also left enough material for future growth over a projected 15-year life cycle.

During the design process, engineers looked at over 30 different valvetrain arrangements, using two, three, and four valves per cylinder and multiple cams. They even brought in some vintage 426 Hemi parts to study valve angles and how those heads flowed. To gain even more insight into the Hemi design, a few retirees were contacted and interviewed. No stone was left unturned in the process.

One major advantage of the Hemi engine architecture is its ability to conduct airflow into the combustion chamber. The 426 Hemi had an included valve angle of 58.5 degrees. From a packaging standpoint, that was not going to work with the new 5.7-liter Hemi. The design team worked on several different designs to get the best compromise between packaging and airflow and

came up with a 34.5-degree included valve angle. This valve angle gave engineers some charge motion within the cylinder that wasn't ideal. To remedy the situation, they added some shape to the inside of the combustion chambers. This changed the combustion characteristics and greatly improved the emissions. But they needed to increase the cylinder's burn rate.

In 2003, Dodge introduced the 5.7-liter, 345-horsepower Hemi engine for its Ram truck line. The Society of Automotive Engineers (SAE) establishes how automobile companies can determine the rating of an engine for advertising purposes. That standard states that the engine must be rated with all the accessories that it would normally have as installed in a vehicle. Previous standards allowed for different levels of engine dress. For example, the 426 Hemi was rated with a standard that was called "lab gross." That standard allowed for a different set of conditions, and with that standard, the 426 Hemi was rated at 425 horsepower. Today, if it were run on that old standard, the new 5.7-liter Hemi engine would develop 392 horsepower instead of its rated 345 horsepower. No matter how it was rated, this new Hemi engine quickly established class-leading performance in the Ram pickup truck. Even though it is 4 percent smaller in displacement, the engine produces 41 percent more power than the 5.9-liter engine it replaced. This third-generation Hemi engine upholds Chrysler's reputation for engineering excellence.

Shortly after the release of the new Hemi-equipped Ram pickup, the designers at Performance West looked back at Dodge's performance history and created this Rumble Bee concept. Chrysler liked it so much they created a limited edition Rumble Bee for their dealers.

Rumble Bee

The Dodge Ram pickup is a great looking truck. But Larry Weiner, head of the Performance West Group, a company that builds image vehicles for Chrysler, envisioned something that borrowed from a historical Dodge muscle car and blended it with the new Hemi-powered pickup. His creation is the Rumble Bee.

The 1960s-era muscle cars were all about power and image, and there were no limits on the size of the engine, the speed, the colors, or the graphics. That's the feeling Weiner intended to create with the new Hemi-powered Rumble Bee. He conceived the Rumble Bee as a salute to the Super Bee's contribution to the muscle car era. The Rumble Bee starts with a Ram 1500 standard cab, short bed, and is equipped with a 345-horsepower, 5.7-liter Hemi. Weiner's Performance West Group added a Kenne Bell 2.2-

In 1970, the Dodge Super Bee featured "C" side stripes with the famous Super Bee logo. The 2005 Rumble Bee stripes are reminiscent of that original design. The paint on the Hemi Rumble Bee is called SpectraFlair B-5 Blue. The wheels are highly polished Oasis "M1" Alloy Wheels that mount BFGoodrich g-Force T/A KDW tires.

liter Blowzilla Supercharger and Intercooler that boosted the Hemi's output to over 500 horsepower.

The Dodge Hemi Rumble Bee rides on BF Goodrich g-Force T/A KDW tires mated with Oasis "M1" Alloy Wheels. Just like the 1969 Super Bees, Performance West's Rumble Bee has a black, Six Pack–inspired hood. The paint on this special Dodge Hemi Rumble Bee is a unique SpectraFlair B-5 Blue, accented with a classic interpretation of the original Super Bee graphic "C" stripe in white.

Providing the rumble for the Rumble Bee concept is a Kenne Bell Blowzilla Supercharger and an intercooler that increases the Hemi's output to over 500 tire-shredding horsepower.

In addition to a set of custom lowering springs, the stance of the Hurst 300 is enhanced by a set of Oasis 22-inch diameter wheels with low-profile Toyo performance tires. Behind the wheels are 13.5-inch diameter drilled and slotted rotors and three-piston calipers manufactured by Stainless Steel.

Dodge executives liked Performance West Group's Rumble Bee concept so much they asked if they could turn it into a production vehicle. In the spring of 2004, Dodge shipped the first Rumble Bees to dealers. Dodge produced the Dodge Ram 1500 Rumble Bees in two colors: black or Solar Yellow. Designers added the contrasting bumblebee stripes across the rear of the bed in either Solar Yellow or black with the Rumble Bee logo. In addition to the 345-horsepower Hemi engine, Dodge added a body-color hood scoop, brushed aluminum fuel filler door, body-color taillight guards, and chrome exhaust tip. Available as an option are 20-inch diameter polished aluminum wheels. The response was overwhelming, and Dodge quickly sold several thousand Rumble Bees.

Chrysler C300 and Magnum

While the new Hemi engine was in its final stages of development for Dodge trucks, the engineers at Chrysler were working on a new full-size vehicle to replace its aging LH front-wheel-drive platform. Discussions began as early as 1998 in an effort to identify the next big thing that could take Chrysler well into the next decade. One of the main forces for change was the overworked look of the long front overhang on a front-wheel-drive vehicle. A new car should have new proportions. For both aesthetic and functional reasons, Chrysler decided its new LX platform should be rear-wheel drive. The LX four-door sedan would be the new

Chrysler 300, and the station wagon version would be branded as a Dodge.

The new 5.7-liter Hemi was being developed within a time frame that would support the new LX program. But to avoid getting hit with the gas guzzler tax, this new vehicle had to get at least 22.5 miles per gallon. To reach the new car's mileage goals, the MDS (Multiple Displacement System) for the Hemi engine was required.

When Chrysler's engineers created the new 5.7-liter Hemi engine, they had the MDS in mind. They knew that although the

The Chrysler 300's stock Hemi engine provides enough power to spin even the widest tires. Performance West worked its magic on the new 300C when it created the Hurst 300. They kept the stock grille, but modified it by removing all the vertical bars except for the center one.

average customer desired a performance vehicle, this customer would rarely use the vehicle's performance capabilities in daily driving. It is the manufacturer's job to satisfy the customer's desire for power and performance and somehow deal with the fuel economy consequences. Multi-displacement systems had been tried years ago but were not well executed. The difference today is the amount of computing power available to manage such complex systems.

Because of today's computing power, Chrysler can predict what the engine will do in 4-cylinder mode and what it will do in 8-cylinder mode. With this computer capability, they manage that transition with electronic throttle control. When the engine is shifting from 4 to 8 cylinders, there is quite a bit going on, such as the spark advance changing very dramatically as the throttle is being repositioned. The bottom line is that Chrysler succeeded in integrating the MDS to create a seamless transition between 4- and 8-cylinder modes without the driver ever being able to detect any difference.

The Hemi engine's computer and control system models are constantly running. This permits cylinders to be switched off and on within a given cycle, the duration of which is 40 milliseconds (0.040 seconds). When the cylinder is deactivated, the system traps an inert exhaust charge. The deactivation is accomplished by means of special hydraulic lifters that collapse to a point where the valves in

the deactivated cylinders are completely closed. The trapped exhaust charge acts like an air spring within the cylinder; as the piston runs up and down, it compresses and expands the trapped charge.

Matching a completely new engine to a completely new car introduces a high level of complexity and risk. Chrysler's engineers took on the complexity, while management assumed the risk. Chrysler's choice of transmission to back the Hemi in the LX platform was made easier thanks to the merger with Mercedes. The five-speed WA580 that Mercedes Benz had been using for years packaged exceptionally well behind the Hemi. The integration of this transmission required the construction of a new transmission plant in Kokomo, Indiana.

Automobile designers are obsessed with the stance of a vehicle. One of the things that most enhances a car's stance is an aggressive set of wheels and the correct tires. At the start of the program, Chrysler's design office wanted to offer 20-inch wheels on the new LX cars. The engineering group counter-offered 16-inch tires. Larger wheels mean wider tires. The larger the wheel, the more difficult it is to package, especially when it comes to engineering a tight turning diameter. Selecting wheels and tires is a difficult balancing act to satisfy the demands of appearance and functionality. Chrysler decided upon an 18-inch diameter wheel for the 300C and Dodge Magnum RT. The wheel is fitted with a 225/60 R18 99H Continental tire.

With the packaging for the new Chrysler 300C and Dodge Magnum well underway, Chrysler's design office started working to identify and establish the look of the classic American car. Tom Gale was still running the program at that time, and they had just brought in Freeman Thomas as Vice President of Advanced Design.

Dodge's version of Chrysler's new LX platform is the Magnum. Four-wheel disc brakes are standard on all Dodge Magnum models. Cooling ducts have been added to the front fascia to direct air to the front calipers.

With its deeply tunneled gauges, the Dodge Magnum's instrument panel bears a striking resemblance to the Dodge Viper's instrument panel. The steering wheel's four spokes are trimmed with silver accents. This Magnum has an optional navigation system as well as satellite radio.

Initially, they conducted studies on a variety of vehicles, looking for different proportions. "There was a lot of talk about *not* just doing another rear-wheel-drive vehicle," says John Opfer, senior designer, who worked in the Advanced Studio. "By that I mean there are competitive rear-wheel-drive vehicles in the American market, but we didn't feel that there had been anything done that was a real 'stand out' or that had taken advantage of the opportunities that they could have with the rear-wheel-drive architecture. We looked at a variety of vehicles, and what finally resonated was the 1955 Chrysler C300."

The most direct lineage to the new 300C can be seen in the 1998 Chrysler Chronos show car. The Chronos had a high beltline with full, rounded wheel openings. In the front, the large egg crate grille stood out as the dominant focal point, as does the grille on the 300C.

The new 300C and Dodge Magnum have unique proportions, not seen before on an American production car. The roofs are low and look as though they have been customized by George Barris in the style of a chopped 1949 Mercury. In doing so, Chrysler's designers created a car that appears fresh, uniquely American, and highly identifiable.

Chrysler's LX body engineers were able to build an attractive, different station wagon in the Dodge Magnum. It delivers the benefits of a sport utility vehicle with the comfort of a passenger car and the performance of a 1960s-era muscle car. The Chrysler LX designers once again veered off the straight and narrow path to offer a new twist on an old design. The large cargo opening is accessed through a rear tailgate door that is hinged midway between the C- and D-pillars. This brilliant design solution gives unprecedented access because of the large opening.

The new Hemi-powered 300C and Dodge Magnum RT are wonderful cars to look at and to drive. Each will reach 60 miles per hour in less than 6 seconds and run the quarter mile in 14.1 seconds at 101 miles per hour. These are elapsed times and speeds of a vintage Road Runner. The 300C will reach its chip-limited 126 miles per hour in a heartbeat and cruise there without whimpering. It is quiet around town, but when the pedal hits the floor, the 5.7-liter Hemi sounds like a Hemi.

Dodge Charger

With the new LX platform, Dodge saw an opportunity to create another car that connects with its past. For 2006, Dodge released the Charger. Its bold fender lines are suggestive of the 1960s era Chargers. Chrysler calls the grille a "crosshair" design, and that's exactly where they see the competition—in the crosshairs. Dodge released five different versions of the new Charger. The SE and SXT are both powered by the 250-horsepower, 3.5-liter V-6. The R/T, Daytona R/T, and SRT8 all have the new Hemi in various

For 2006, Dodge added a Daytona version of its new Charger. This one is painted Top Banana Yellow. The only other available color is Go Mango Bronze. Dodge is limiting production to 4,000 units in each of these bold colors. The wing is the same one used on the SRT8 Charger.

The Charger's two sneering headlight eyes and a bold blacked-out crosshair grille distinguish it as a car to be reckoned with. On the lower right-hand corner of the grille is an R/T badge. Dodge added fog lamps as a standard component of the 2005 Charger Daytona option.

The engine cover on the Charger Daytona has its center panel painted Hemi Orange. The Charger Daytona's 345-horsepower Hemi engine does not require premium unleaded gas.

levels of tune. The R/T includes aggressive 18-inch wheels and R/T badging. The Daytona R/T version also includes 18-inch wheels along with a performance-tuned dual exhaust system and a special front fascia and rear deck lid spoiler. Dodge has also added unique body-colored interior accents and exterior decal graphics in black. The familiar "HEMI" is on the hood and distinctive "Daytona" lettering is on the quarter panel.

The new Charger has its fans and detractors. Some feel that Dodge should not have produced the Charger as a four-door model, that it should have been a two-door just like the original. But times have changed. In the 1960s, two-door hardtops and convertibles were the only models seen in the sporty performance category; anything with four doors was labeled as a grocery-getter or grandpa's Sunday driving car. Four-door cars of the 1960s were boxy and unattractive. They were practical and homely to a fault. But throughout the 1990s, auto stylists improved the design of four-door cars. Instead of putting a box on top of a bigger box, today's designers tightly integrated the body and roof into one flowing shape. Also, the American customer had come to realize that four doors were practical, especially with kids. Europe's top performance sedans have been built with four doors for years. So it was only natural that the new Charger would have four doors.

Chrysler's SRT team of engineers enhanced the already aggressive-looking Dodge Charger by adding a functional scoop to the hood. The SRT8 Charger sits approximately 1/2 inch lower than the standard Charger.

Chrysler's solution to the two-door Hemi-powered image car was also in the works and would be introduced at the 2006 Detroit International Auto Show.

SRT8: Magnum, 300C, and Charger

With the knowledge that Chrysler was going to bring out a new rear-wheel-drive car with a Hemi V-8, engineers at Chrysler's SRT (Street & Racing Technology) group must have been like kids waiting for Christmas morning. Chrysler's SRT team had already cut its performance teeth on the Viper SRT10, Viper-powered Dodge Ram SRT10, Crossfire SRT6, and the Neon SRT4; now they could work their magic on the latest-generation Chrysler Hemi engine and an exciting new vehicle.

The new SRT8s would be a complete package, just like every performance car Chrysler has ever built in its long performance history. Nothing would be overlooked or left out, and everything would work together in complete harmony.

The heart of the SRT8 package is the new Hemi engine. In stock trim, this engine develops an honest 345 horsepower. That engine is more than adequate for the average street driven car, but not quite adequate for one badged "SRT"—the new Hemi for the SRT8 develops 425 horsepower, just like the legendary 426 Hemi.

But when Chrysler's engineers designed the new Hemi engine they left plenty of room for growth. For the SRT8

Hemi, they increased the displacement to 370 cubic inches (6.1 liters) by enlarging the bore to 4.00 inches. Then they increased the compression ratio to 10.3:1 and added a hotter camshaft. New high-flow heads were added to match up to the new intake manifold's big diameter runners. The engine's tubular exhaust headers are connected to a free flowing 2.75-inch diameter exhaust system. In homage to the original Hemi, Chrysler's product planners made sure that the SRT8's valve covers were black and that the engine block was painted Hemi Orange.

The SRT8 package includes an upgraded chassis. The improvements include special springs and shocks along with large diameter sway bars. The ride height of the SRT8 car is 1/2 inch lower than its standard counterparts. Chrysler's SRT group developed a special set of 20-inch diameter forged aluminum wheels that are fitted with Goodyear Supercar F1 tires, 245/45/20 in the front and 255/45/20 in the rear. Behind those wheels is a massive set of Brembo four-piston brakes and vented rotors.

Any one of the three SRT8 cars will accelerate from 0 to 60 in 5.25 seconds, and they will run the quarter mile in 13.6 seconds at 105 miles per hour. With the traction control turned off, it takes only a twitch of the right foot to light up the rear tires. The SRT8s have the wheel-spinning performance and booming sound of the original Hemi. This superb muscle car performance is wrapped up

Powering DaimlerChrysler's SRT-optioned 300, Magnum, or Charger is this 425-horsepower, 370-cubic-inch (6.1-liter) version of the new Hemi engine. Designers even added black valve covers and painted the block Hemi Orange.

The special aluminum wheels fitted to the Dodge Charger SRT8 are 20 inches in diameter and 9 inches wide. They mount Goodyear high-performance Z-rated tires. A massive set of Brembo four-piston calipers with vented rotors provides the Charger SRT8's stopping power.

in a beautiful package that can handle like a sports car and even get decent mileage. We expect more out of today's cars, especially those billed as performance models. Chrysler has certainly delivered with the SRT8s by setting a high benchmark for the modern American muscle car.

Challenger Concept

At the 2006 Detroit International Auto Show, Dodge kicked off a tornado of excitement that swirled around its bold new Challenger concept—it seemed to be the most photographed and written about car at the show. It created a firestorm of anticipation among Mopar enthusiasts who all hoped that Dodge would actually produce another generation of pony cars with the same personality and performance as the original Challengers.

Chrysler's designers at its West Coast Pacifica Design Studios were tasked with creating a Dodge Challenger concept car. This kind of project could have been a career-ending move if the results didn't ring true with the legions of Mopar fans eagerly awaiting a new Challenger. The new Challenger had to look like a *Challenger*, not a Neon with Challenger emblems.

Chrysler assigned Michael Castiglione as the principal designer in charge of the exterior and Alan Barrington as the

designer in charge of the interior. They saw the 1970 Challenger as the "icon" of the Challenger models and actually brought one into the studio for inspiration. Their goal was not to copy the original Challenger line for line, but to capture the "essence" of the original Challenger. They wanted to reproduce the image that one sees in the mind's eye when thinking of a Challenger.

Initially, three proposals were produced for the concept car, but only Castiglione's design had a retro theme. "We did three scale models about mid '04," says Castiglione. "Mine was the most literal interpretation of the original car, and the other two were more advanced cars done by other designers. Those two were actually chosen to go full size, and mine was dropped at that point." Chrysler worked on the development of those two versions. But during that time period, the new Charger was introduced and the negative feedback Chrysler received because of its four-door body style and lack of a manual transmission made them rethink their decision to drop the retro version. "They decided to go back with a little more retro approach," says Castiglione. "This brought my car back to the surface."

Chrysler management wanted to use the LX platform as the basis for this new car. But its 120-inch wheelbase was too big for the proportions of the new Challenger. To establish the proper

The hottest car at the 2006 Detroit International Auto Show was Dodge's Challenger concept. It has all the flavor of the original Challenger, plus the new Hemi engine.

This photo was taken at Chrysler's Pacifica Design Studio on April 25, 2005, one month prior to the finalization of the design. The designers brought in several vintage Challengers to be sure they had captured the essence of the original design in the concept vehicle.

proportions, they had to shorten the wheelbase by 4 inches. Because of cost issues, they had to retain the LX platform's engine box and cowl. This locked in the point at which the windshield meets the cowl, which is quite a bit farther forward than the original. "If you look at them in dead side view," says Castiglione, "the windshield is much farther forward than on the original." The result is that the Challenger's concept hood is also about a foot shorter than on the original Challenger. "It was a challenge to make the cab look like it's tucked back really rearward on the car," says Castiglione. "We did as many tricks as we could to maintain the proportions." One of those tricks was to pull the side mirror rearward, thereby emphasizing the hood.

Another design problem that was difficult to work out was the height of the platform. "The LX is considered a 'tall-car' platform that has a great command of the road and a good seating position," says Castiglione. "We couldn't change that; we had to make this car look super low and super wide like a '70 Challenger."

The proportion design elements that Castiglione changed were mostly in side view. "A signature of recent Chrysler designs is the thick body with a squat-looking upper and sort of a chopped-looking roof," says Castiglione. "We wanted to maintain that signature because it has really gotten picked up by the public. So the body is a lot chunkier and the roofs are a little lower than the original car." They also widened the rear track and added deep-dish wheels.

Alan Barrington's interior also carries a retro theme. In 1970, the Mopar E-body 'Cudas and Challengers had an interior that was distinctly different than the Camaro or Mustang, and Barrington wanted to capture that feeling. "The 'Cuda and Challenger both had a pretty unique center console that had an asymmetrical design," says Barrington. "I wanted to revisit that in a new way." In 1970, Chrysler designers added a trapezoidal surround to the iconic Pistol Grip shifter. It also leaned toward the driver to give more of a command feel. Barrington created a similarly shaped console for the Challenger concept, but for a modern touch he

Chrysler's excellent LX platform provides the foundation for the Challenger concept. To preserve the proportions of the vehicle, it had to be shortened by four inches.

The Challenger concept's Tuff-styled steering wheel and asymmetrical console are all references to the original Challenger. The pistol grip shifter was updated from the revolver style of the 1970s to a more modern 9mm automatic–style grip.

added a pistol grip shifter in the shape of a more modern 9mm automatic, instead of a vintage revolver-style handle.

In 1970, Chrysler added molded door trim panels to the new 'Cudas and Challengers. At that time, they were the state of the art in automobile interior design. Today, they look more cut-rate than high-zoot. "I wanted to revisit that in a new modern way that's a lot more precise with newer materials and forms," says Barrington. The door panels he created have the look of the originals, but are highly refined with a more modern inspiration to them.

The color of any concept car is critical. The manufacturer has one chance to make an impression, and selecting the right color is exceptionally important. "Originally I wanted to do SubLime [lime green]," says Castiglione. "Because I thought that was the most signature color back in the day, and no one else had anything close to that color." Chrysler's color studio did a survey at Daytona Raceway where SubLime rated very low. Another reason the color folks didn't like SubLime is because it photographs poorly. The other signature color from the 1970s that Castiglione considered was Plum Crazy (purple). "We had one shot at making an impression with the car, and I didn't want to use anything feminine," says Castiglione. "I wanted the car to be very masculine. My second choice was orange. It's a distinct muscle car color, and we did have a history with that color, too." This is also a masculine color that looks exceptionally nice with black accents.

In June 2006, DaimlerChrysler announced that the new Dodge Challenger would be available to anxious customers in early 2008. This news was met with enthusiastic approval by the

Designer Micheal Castiglione did this sketch of the Challenger concept in Plum Crazy (purple)—one of the signature Mopar muscle car colors of the 1970s. This color received strong consideration for the show car.

legions of avid Mopar fans. Today, the Mustang owns the pony car market. Ford's latest version of its legendary pony car is the best it's ever produced. Chevrolet introduced its Camaro concept at the 2006 Detroit Auto Show, but it didn't create the same buzz as the Challenger concept. With its new Challenger, Dodge is in an excellent position to capitalize on this strong pony car market segment. They have the proven LX platform and the powerful new Hemi engine to anchor the project. They also have a corporate mindset that understands what an icon of the muscle car era the original Challenger has become, and not to use that imagery would be an insult to the Challenger's heritage.

JEEP SRT8: 415 HEMI HORSEPOWER

DaimlerChrysler's all new 2006 Jeep Grand Cherokee SRT8 is the ultimate performance sports utility vehicle. Its SRT-engineered 6.1-liter Hemi engine, along with its specially developed full-time four-wheel-drive system, gives it stunning performance.

Powering the Jeep Grand Cherokee SRT8 is a 6.1-liter Hemi engine producing 415 horsepower and 410 ft-lb of torque. The Jeep rockets to 60 miles per hour in fewer than 5 seconds and runs 0–100 miles per hour in the low 19-second range. The performance of the Jeep Grand Cherokee SRT8 is equal to or better than that of the Porsche Cayenne Turbo at half the price.

To handle the high levels of horsepower and torque that the Hemi produces, the SRT team had to develop a reliable full-time four-wheel-drive system. Engineers created a new transfer case by combining the components from two existing units. They married the front half of the standard Jeep transfer case to a heavy-duty rear half that houses the electronic full-time four-wheel-drive.

SRT engineers opted to use the front half of a standard Jeep transfer case because of its capability and light weight. They mated it to the rear half of a heavy-duty Jeep case, selected for its ruggedness and ability to house the electronic full-time four-wheel-drive system components. They then upgraded the transfer case output shaft to handle the Hemi's high torque. This new transfer case weighs 60 pounds less than the heavy-duty Jeep version. This sophisticated system directs 5 to 10 percent of the torque to the front wheels during normal driving conditions. It can direct more as needed when additional traction or stability is required. This SRT-developed electronic four-wheel-drive system gives the driver an exceptionally well-balanced vehicle under all driving conditions.

To compliment the Hemi engine and full-time four-wheel-drive, Chrysler's SRT engineers balanced the Jeep Grand Cherokee SRT8's chassis with SRT-tuned dampers, unique sway bars, and unique tailored spring rates. These new springs give the 2006 Jeep Grand Cherokee SRT8 a ride height that is one inch lower than the standard Jeep Grand Cherokee. Adding to the aggressive stance established by the springs is a set of 20-inch diameter forged five-spoke aluminum wheels fitted with Goodyear W-rated tires. Behind those wheels are gloss black four-piston Brembo brake calipers that work in conjunction with vented rotors, front and rear.

To explain the impressive performance of the SRT8 Jeep Grand Cherokee is Jim Nelson, half of the Dragmaster team of Nelson and Martin and the race driver who drove the Dragmaster Dart to a Top Eliminator win at the 1962 NHRA Winternationals. This is a man who understands performance. I picked him up at his house for an event at the NHRA Museum. I drove the SRT8 Jeep Grand Cherokee conservatively until I got to the freeway entrance ramp—then I nailed it. Jim's eyes opened wide, and he yelled, "Whooah, this sucker can run!"

EARLY HEMI ENGINES 1951–1958

Year	Cubic Inch Dis	Horsepower	Torque	BorexStroke	Compression	Carb	Intake Valve dia	Exhaust Valve Dia	Notes
1951	331	180@4,000	312@2,000	3.81x3.63	7.5:1	2 barrel	1.81	1.50	First production Chrysler Hemi—extended bellhousing
1952	331	180@4,000	312@2,000	3.81x3.63	7.5:1	2 barrel	1.81	1.50	Chrysler same as 1951 engine
1952	276	160@4,400	250@2,000	3.63x3.34	7.0:1	2 barrel	1.84	1.50	DeSoto FireDome
1953	331	180@4,000	312@2,000	3.81x3.63	7.5:1	2 barrel	1.81	1.50	Chrysler FirePower
1953	276	160@4,400	250@2,000	3.63x3.34	7.1:1	2 barrel	1.84	1.50	DeSoto FireDome
1953	241	140@4,400	220@2,000	3.44x3.25	7.0:1	2 barrel	1.75	1.41	Dodge Red Ram
1954	331	195@4,000	320@2,000	3.81x3.63	7.5:1	2 barrel	1.81	1.50	Chrysler FirePower
1954	331	235@4,400	330@2,600	3.81x3.63	7.5:1	4 barrel	1.81	1.50	Chrysler FirePower first 4-barrel Hemi
1954	276	170@4,400	255@2,400	3.63x3.34	7.5:1	2 barrel	1.84	1.50	DeSoto FireDome
1954	241	140@4,400	220@2,000	3.44x3.25	7.1:1	2 barrel	1.75	1.41	Dodge Red Ram
1955	331	250@4,600	340@2,800	3.81x3.63	8.5:1	4 barrel	1.94	1.50	Chrysler FirePower also used in Imperial
1955	331	300@5,200	345@3,200	3.81x3.63	8.5:1	two 4 barrel	1.94	1.50	Chrysler C300
1955	291	180@4,400	245@2,800	3.72x3.34	7.5:1	2 barrel	1.84	1.50	DeSoto FireFlite
1955	291	200@4,400	274@2,800	3.72x3.34	7.5:1	4 barrel	1.84	1.50	DeSoto FireDome
1955	270	183@4,400	245@2,400	3.63x3.25	7.6:1	2 barrel	1.75	1.41	Dodge Red Ram
1955	270	193@4,400	245@2,400	3.63x3.25	7.6:1	4 barrel	1.75	1.41	Dodge Red Ram
1956	354	280@4,600	380@2,800	3.94x3.63	9.0:1	4 barrel	1.94	1.75	Chrysler & Imperial
1956	354	340@5,200	385@3,200	3.94x3.63	9.0:1	two 4 barrel	1.94	1.75	Chrysler 300B
1956	354	355@5,200	————-	3.94x3.63	10.0:1	two 4 barrel	1.94	1.75	Chrysler 300B racing
1956	330	230@4,400	305@2,800	3.72x3.80	8.5:1	2 barrel	1.94	1.75	DeSoto FireDome
1956	330	255@4,400	350@3,200	3.72x3.80	8.5:1	4 barrel	1.94	1.75	DeSoto FireFlite
1956	341	320@5,200	356@4,000	3.78x3.80	9.5:1	two 4 barrel	1.94	1.75	DeSoto Adventurer
1956	315	260@4,800	330@3,000	3.63x3.80	9.25:1	4 barrel	1.87	1.53	Dodge Red Ram
1956	315	295@5,000	————-	3.63x3.80	9.25:1	two 4 barrel	1.87	1.53	Dodge Red Ram
1957	392	325@4,600	430@2,800	4.00x3.91	9.25:1	4 barrel	2.00	1.75	Chrysler & Imperial
1957	392	375@5,200	430@2,800	4.00x3.91	9.25:1	two 4 barrel	2.00	1.75	Chrysler 300C
1957	341	270@4,600	270@3,600	3.78x3.80	9.25:1	2 barrel	1.94	1.75	DeSoto FireDome
1957	341	295@4,600	295@3,600	3.78x3.80	9.25:1	4 barrel	1.94	1.75	DeSoto FireFlite
1957	345	345@5,200	355@3,600	3.80x3.80	9.5:1	two 4 barrel	1.94	1.75	DeSoto Adventurer
1957	325	285@4,800	345@2,800	3.69x3.80	9.25:1	4 barrel	1.87	1.53	Dodge Red Ram
1957	325	310@5,000	350@3,200	3.69x3.80	9.25:1	two 4 barrel	1.87	1.53	Dodge Red Ram
1957	354	340@5,200	385@3,200	3.94x3.63	9.0:1	two 4 barrel	1.94	1.75	Dodge Export (1956 Chrysler 300B engine)
1957	354	355@5,200	————-	3.94x3.63	10.0:1	two 4 barrel	1.94	1.75	Dodge Racing (1956 Chrysler 300B racing engine)
1958	392	345@4,600	450@2,800	4.00x3.91	10:1	4 barrel	2.00	1.75	Chrysler & Imperial
1958	392	380@5,200	435@3,600	4.00x3.91	10:1	two 4 barrel	2.00	1.75	Chrysler 300D
1958	392	390@5,200	————-	4.00x3.91	10:1	F.I.	2.00	1.75	Chrysler 300D (Bendix electronic fuel injection)